Everyman's Poetry

Everyman, I will go with th…
and be th…

William Shakespeare

Selected and edited by MARTIN DODSWORTH

Royal Holloway, University of London

This edition first published by Everyman Paperbacks in 1996

J. M. Dent
Orion Publishing Group
Orion House
5 Upper St Martin's Lane
London WC2H 9EA

Typeset by Deltatype Ltd, Birkenhead, Merseyside
Printed in Great Britain by
The Guernsey Press Co. Ltd, Guernsey, C.I.

British Library Cataloguing-in-Publication
Data is available upon request.

ISBN 0 460 87815 8

Contents

Note on the Author and Editor

WILLIAM SHAKESPEARE is held to have been born on St George's day, 23 April 1564. The eldest son of a prosperous glove-maker in Stratford-upon-Avon, he was probably educated at the town's grammar school.

Tradition holds that between 1585 and 1592, Shakespeare first became a schoolteacher and then set off for London. By 1595 he was a leading member of the Lord Chamberlain's Men, helping to direct their business affairs, as well as being a playwright and actor. In 1598 he became a part-owner of the company, which was the most distinguished of its age. However, he maintained his contacts with Stratford, and his family seem to have remained there.

From about 1610 he seems to have grown increasingly involved in the town's affairs, suggesting a withdrawal from London. He died on 23 April 1616, on his fifty-second birthday, and was buried at Holy Trinity Church two days later.

MARTIN DODSWORTH, is Professor of English at Royal Holloway, University of London. He is the author of *Hamlet Closely Observed* (1985) and editor of *The Survival of Poetry* (1970), *English Economis'd* (1989) and *The Penguin History of Literature* Vol. 7: *The Twentieth Century* (1994). He has been Chairman and President of The English Association. For many years he reviewed contemporary poetry for *The Guardian*.

Chronology of Shakespeare's Life

Year[1]	*Age*	*Life*
1564		Shakespeare baptized 26 April at Stratford-upon-Avon
1582	18	Marries Anne Hathaway
1583	19	Daughter, Susanna, born
1585	21	Twin son and daughter, Hamnet and Judith, born
1590–1	26	*The Two Gentlemen of Verona & The Taming of the Shrew*
1591	27	*2 & 3 Henry VI*
1592	28	*Titus Andronicus & I Henry VI*
1592–3		*Richard III*
1593	29	*Venus and Adonis* published
1594	30	*The Comedy of Errors. The Rape of Lucrece* published
1594–5		*Love's Labour's Lost*

Chronology of his Times

Year	*Artistic Events*	*Historical Events*
1565–7	Golding, Ovid's *Metamorphoses*, tr.	Elizabeth I reigning
1574	*A Mirror for Magistrates* (3rd ed.)	
1576	London's first playhouse built	
1578	John Lyly, *Euphues*	
1579	North, Plutarch's *Lives*, tr.	
	Spenser, *Shepheardes Calender*	
1587	Marlowe, *I Tamburlaine*	Mary Queen of Scots executed
	Holinshed's *Chronicles* (2nd ed.)	Defeat of Spanish Armada
1589	Kyd, *Spanish Tragedy*	Civil war in France
	Marlowe, *Jew of Malta*	
1590	Spenser, *Faerie Queene*, Bks I–III	
1591	Sidney, *Astrophil and Stella*	Proclamation against Jesuits
1592	Marlowe, *Dr Faustus & Edward II*	Scottish witchcraft trials
		Plague closes theatres from June
1593	Marlowe killed	
1594	Nashe, *Unfortunate Traveller*	Theatres reopen in summer
1594–6		Extreme food shortages

Year	*Age*	*Life*
1595	31	*A Midsummer Night's Dream, Romeo and Juliet, & Richard II.* An established member of Lord Chamberlain's Men
1596	32	*King John.* Hamnet dies
1596–7		*The Merchant of Venice & I Henry IV*
1597	33	Buys New Place in Stratford The Lord Chamberlain's Men's lease to play at the Theatre expires; until 1599 they play mainly at the Curtain
1597–8		*The Merry Wives of Windsor & 2 Henry IV*
1598	34	*Much Ado About Nothing*
1598–9		*Henry V*
1599	35	*Julius Caesar.* One of syndicate responsible for building the Globe in Southwark, where the Lord Chamberlain's Men now play
1599–1600		*As You Like It*
1600–1		*Hamlet*
1601	37	*Twelfth Night.* His father is buried in Stratford
1602	38	*Troilus and Cressida.* Invests £320 in land near Stratford[2]
1603	39	*Measure for Measure.* The Lord Chamberlain's Men become the King's Men. They play at court more than all the other companies combined
1603–4		*Othello*
c. 1604	40	Shakespeare sues Philip Rogers of Stratford for debt
1604–5		*All's Well that Ends Well*
1605	41	*Timon of Athens.* Invests £440 in Stratford tithes
1605–6		*King Lear*
1606	42	*Macbeth & Antony and Cleopatra*
1607	43	*Pericles.* Susanna marries the physician John Hall in Stratford

Year	*Artistic Events*	*Historical Events*
1595	Sidney, *An Apologie for Poetry*	Riots in London
1596		Calais captured by Spanish Cádiz expedition
1597	Bacon's *Essays*	
1598	Marlowe and Chapman, *Hero and Leander* Jonson, *Every Man in his Humour*	Rebellion in Ireland
1599	Children's companies begin playing Thomas Dekker's *Shoemaker's Holiday*	Essex fails in Ireland
1601	'War of the Theatres' Jonson, *Poetaster*	Essex rebels and is executed
1602		Tyrone defeated in Ireland
1603	Florio, Montaigne's *Essays*, tr.	Elizabeth I dies, James I accedes Raleigh found guilty of treason
1604	Marston, *The Malcontent*	Peace with Spain
1605	Bacon's *Advancement of Learning*	Gunpowder plot
1606	Jonson's *Volpone*	
1607	Tourneur's *The Revenger's Tragedy*, published	Virginia colonized Enclosure riots

Year	*Age*	*Life*
1608	44	*Coriolanus*. The King's Men lease Blackfriars, an indoor theatre. His only grandchild is born. His mother dies
1609	45	*The Winter's Tale*. 'Sonnets' and 'A Lover's Complaint' published
1610	46	*Cymbeline*
1611	47	*The Tempest*
1613	49	*Henry VIII*. Buys house in London for £140
1613–14		*The Two Noble Kinsmen*
1616	52	Judith marries Thomas Quiney, a vintner, in Stratford. On 23 April he dies, and is buried two days later
1623	59	Publication of the First Folio. His wife dies in August

[1] It is rarely possible to be certain about the dates at which plays of this period were written. For Shakespeare's plays, this chronology follows the dates preferred by Wells and Taylor, the editors of the Oxford Shakespeare. Publication dates are given for poetry and books.

[2] A schoolmaster would earn around £20 a year at this time.

Year	*Artistic Events*	*Historical Events*
1609		Oath of allegiance Truce in Netherlands
1610	Jonson, *Alchemist*	
1611	Authorized Version of the Bible Donne, *Anatomy of the World*	
1612	Webster, *White Devil*	Prince Henry dies
1613	Webster, *Duchess of Malfi*	Princess Elizabeth marries
1614	Jonson, *Bartholomew Fair*	
1616	Folio edition of Jonson's plays	

Biographical note and chronology compiled by John Lee, University of Bristol, 1993.

Introduction

Shakespeare's sonnets were first printed almost four hundred years ago, in 1609. They are some of the greatest poems of love ever written, and there remains about them a striking, even startling, immediacy and simplicity of expression, as a few first lines will show: 'O how I faint when I of you do write . . .'; 'To me, fair friend, you never can be old . . .'; 'O never say that I was false of heart . . .'. Each first line *plunges* us into the poem that follows. But these dramatic openings lead us into poems that are far from simple in themselves. They are intensely poems of the private life and it is a private life of which virtually nothing is known. We do not know to whom the sonnets were addressed and little is known of the circumstances of their publication. This has not prevented a mass of doubtful speculation. Wordsworth thought that with this key of the sonnets Shakespeare unlocked his heart; it is natural that commentators through the ages should have striven to see further into that heart than Shakespeare allows them to, or even, perhaps, permitted himself. Readers have always felt that there lies behind the sonnets an elusive story of momentous significance for their author. Despite that feeling, no more certain truth than that Shakespeare loved an unnamed someone has emerged, and even that truth is called into question by some readers who see the poems as fictions which tell us no more about Shakespeare than his plays do.

Because it is a selection only, this edition of the sonnets may be of service to the reader by not offering the possibility of reading a story. The poems chosen here present themselves as distinct utterances. In 1609 the sequence was concluded by 'A Lover's Complaint'; in that poem a young woman tells of her seduction by a young man as beautiful and gifted as the one to whom and for whom Shakespeare writes in the sonnets. The young woman has been abandoned by her seducer and, pretty plainly, we are meant to look back on the sonnets in the light of this poem and to reconsider the relationship which they portray. In this selection the poems present themselves as simpler things than, viewed in their proper context, they really are. Consequently, it is possible to think more clearly about one sonnet at a time. Even so, the poems will be found to be complex enough and, in their giving voice to complex feelings, satisfying, too.

The fact that this is a generous selection of the sonnets does, however, offer the reader the chance to see some of the significant inter-relationships between poems. There is an uninterrupted sequence from sonnet 53 to sonnet 69 and another from sonnet 71 to sonnet 98. In these sequences, whether by chance or design, each poem sets off the next. Sonnets 53 to 55 can show something of what is involved in this sequencing. Sonnet 53 is about the young man's beauty and its reflection in everything else that is beautiful – people (Adonis, Helen) and things (spring and autumn in their different characters); Sonnet 54 is about the constancy that makes beauty all the more to be treasured; Sonnet 55 is about the poet's verse in which that treasure will repose and live, even after the friend's death. Sonnet 53 is linked to Sonnet 54 by the reference to constancy in its last line ('But you like none, none you, for constant heart') and Sonnets 54 to 55 by the reference to poetry in its last line ('by verse distils your truth'). The point is not simply that these poems lead on to each other, but that they do so in interesting ways that show up the fluctuation of feeling which is part of the business of love. In Sonnet 53 the tone is one of wonder ('What is your substance, whereof are you made . . . ?') and pride in the young man's constancy capping the triumph of his beauty; in Sonnet 54, at the same time that the poet ups the stakes of praise, a note of doubt insinuates itself in the one small word *seem*:

> O, how much more doth beauty beauteous seem
> By that sweet ornament which truth doth give!

These lines do two things at once – exclaim at how true the young man *is*, and pray that he *may be* so. This sort of unstable elation in love, a willingness to believe against the odds which is itself part of the odds against, is something most people will have experienced. It is here caught in a language uniquely appropriate to the feelings expressed. The emphasis in Sonnet 55 on what the poet's verse can do for the young man seems to follow on naturally as a deflection from thinking about the friend's so-much desired constancy. It seems fitting that in the next sonnet in the sequence Shakespeare should tell love to live in a state of continuous self-renewal:

> Tomorrow see again, and do not kill
> The spirit of love with a perpetual dullness.

To have a sense of how the sonnets read in sequence is to see how they represent a refusal ever to admit to 'dullness'; in them the life that is in love is always working.

This is to write, however, as though the sonnets all made one poem, and that does seem to be an implication of Shakespeare's choosing to end the sonnets with 'A Lover's Complaint' – we shall see later why it is reasonable to think that it was Shakespeare's choice to do so. Yet the sonnets fall rather obviously into three distinct groups, and the dissimilarities between these groups work in a different sense from the evidence of ending with the poem about the abandoned young woman. The first seventeen, of which ten are included here, all seek to persuade a good-looking young man that it is his duty to marry, if for no other reason than that his good looks may be perpetuated. The next one hundred and nine sonnets, of which eighty-three are to be found here, concern the poet's friendship with a 'fair friend' who may or may not be the person to whom the first group is dedicated. The last group of twenty-eight sonnets is concerned largely with the poet's relations with a dark, that is, dark-haired lady. Twelve are printed here.

These three groups are of uneven merit. The first group has a special quality of shimmering formality; the young man is addressed with respect and an admiration that overlays and transforms that respect. The second group forms the heart of the sonnets; here it is difficult to generalize because the poems take such strikingly novel turns. (I have suggested something of their quality in the discussion of sequencing above.) The third group is extremely variable. There is some gross and banal *double-entendre* which is not represented in this selection, an epigrammatic superficiality and tones of disgust, remorse and despair. These poems may be the earliest written of the sonnets, and I have been most willing to reject members of this group, and yet it also contains in Sonnet 129 ('Th'expense of spirit in a waste of shame') one of the finest poems Shakespeare ever wrote.

It is possible to see biographical links between the three groups of sonnets. The young man in the first group may, as I have suggested, be the 'fair friend' of the second and also the 'better angel' of Sonnet 144 in the third group; the dark lady of the last sonnets may be responsible for some of the shame and guilt that we encounter in the middle section. The sonnets, however, are not presented as records of Shakespeare's life, but as examples of his art and memorials of his love. They are best read in that spirit.

Shakespeare's sonnets are part of the craze for the fourteen-line sonnet-form that swept Europe in the sixteenth century and England in particular in the 1590s. Sir Philip Sidney's *Astrophil and Stella*, a set of 108 sonnets and eleven songs, was first published in 1591. It tells the story of Sidney's unsuccessful pursuit of the married Lady Rich, but it does so with only occasional specificity. It gave rise to other sequences, some, like Spenser's *Amoretti* (1595) also alluding to autobiography. Spenser writes about his courtship of, and eventual marriage to, Elizabeth Boyle; others, like Samuel Daniel's *Delia* (1592), apparently have little connection with events in real life.

Shakespeare's sonnets are unusual in being addressed, for the most part, to a man. This fact has traditionally been something of an embarrassment for readers and perhaps explains the inconspicuous place they assumed in accounts of Shakespeare in the seventeenth and eighteenth centuries. When John Benson reprinted them in 1640 he not only rearranged the poems but made them refer to a woman rather than a man. More than a century later the editor George Stevens objected to Sonnet 20 that 'it is impossible to read this fulsome panegyrick, addressed to a male object, without an equal mixture of disgust and indignation'; his more distinguished colleague, Edmund Malone, countered by saying that 'such addresses to men, however indelicate, were customary in our author's time, and neither imported criminality, nor were esteemed indecorous'.

This was the line of argument that prevailed until recently. Scholars pointed to the many representations of fervent friendship between men in the literature of the sixteenth century in order to avoid the imputation that Shakespeare could have had homosexual leanings. Indeed, romances like Sir Philip Sidney's *Arcadia* and plays like Shakespeare's own *Two Gentlemen of Verona* give some plausibility to these palliating accounts. Yet the fact remains that Shakespeare's sonnet-sequence stands out by virtue of its addressing a man, and the association of the sonnet form with autobiography established by Sidney and Spenser makes plausible a specific male friendship in Shakespeare's own life, whether physically consummated or not. It was not unusual for men in the late sixteenth century to share the same bed; at the same time the utmost abhorrence was expressed for any kind of homosexual behaviour. Somewhere in the midst of this contradiction Shakespeare's sonnets were written.

It is not known when the sonnets were written. There is a reference in print to Shakespeare's 'sugared sonnets' in 1598, and in the following year two of them found their way into a collection of poems called *The Passionate Pilgrim*, described as by Shakespeare (though most of the poems it contained were by other authors). The sonnets in *The Passionate Pilgrim* were from the 'dark lady' group and could have been circulating in manuscript for some time before the unscrupulous printer William Jaggard got hold of them. We therefore have no means of dating the bulk of the sonnets and no way of telling, either, whether or not they were revised by their author. What is clear is that Thomas Thorp, the man who printed them in their entirety in 1609, was a reputable businessman who had already printed work for Shakespeare's friend and fellow dramatist Ben Jonson and who had other connections in the world of the theatre. It seems likely, therefore, that the relatively good state of the text of these poems is to be explained by the fact that they came to the printer with their author's blessing. This was not quite so usual a state of affairs in 1609 as might be expected. If Shakespeare authorized the printing of his sonnets in 1609, it is quite possible that he subjected at least some of them to revision before they went to the printing-house.

It was there that Thomas Thorp added his dedication, set out like a Roman inscription and beginning:

TO.THE.ONLIE.BEGETTER.OF.
THESE.INSVING.SONNETS.
M^{r}.W.H.ALL.HAPPINESSE.

Oscar Wilde was far from the only person to identify 'Mr.W.H.' with the young man of Shakespeare's sonnets. There certainly is a link between the word 'begetter' and the subject matter of the opening sonnets which set out to persuade the young man to marry. The sonnets tell us that there was a distance of rank between Shakespeare and his 'fair friend'. Was he, then, William Herbert, third Earl of Pembroke (1580–1630) or (with the initials reversed) Henry Wriothesley, third Earl of Southampton and dedicatee of Shakespeare's poems *Venus and Adonis* and *Lucrece*? We shall never know. Southampton looks a bit old for the part of the young man unless the sonnets were written very early in Shakespeare's career; and Thomas Thorp probably put the dedication in to thank whoever it was that acted as go-between in obtaining for him the manuscript of the sonnets – this would have been consistent with one sense of the word 'begetter'.

These are questions that arise naturally from a reading of the sonnets, but that need not very much disturb a reader of this selection, which is designed to make a first reading of Shakespeare's sonnets a happy experience. I have tried to weed out the less interesting and the more unfortunately clotted of the poems, though any truly understanding reader will want to get beyond a selection and read the whole book eventually. Meanwhile, I can only repeat what Keats had to say about Shakespeare and his sonnets: 'He has left nothing to say about nothing or anything . . .'.

MARTIN DODSWORTH

William Shakespeare

1

From fairest creatures we desire increase,
That thereby beauty's rose might never die,
But as the riper should by time decease,
His tender heir might bear his memory:
But thou, contracted to thine own bright eyes,
Feed'st thy light's flame with self-substantial fuel,
Making a famine where abundance lies,
Thyself thy foe, to thy sweet self too cruel.
Thou that art now the world's fresh ornament
And only herald to the gaudy spring
Within thine own bud buriest thy content,
And, tender churl, mak'st waste in niggarding.
    Pity the world, or else this glutton be,
    To eat the world's due, by the grave and thee.

5 *contracted*] betrothed 10 *gaudy*] bright (no detrimental sense) 12 *mak'st waste in niggarding*] are wasteful by being miserly (with yourself) 14 *the world's due, by the grave and thee*] your children, consumed by you in your self-concern, and by death who consumes you

2

When forty winters shall besiege thy brow
And dig deep trenches in thy beauty's field,
Thy youth's proud livery, so gaz'd on now,
Will be a tatter'd weed of small worth held.
Then being ask'd where all thy beauty lies,
Where all the treasure of thy lusty days,
To say, within thine own deep-sunken eyes
Were an all-eating shame and thriftless praise.
How much more praise deserv'd thy beauty's use,
If thou couldst answer 'This fair child of mine
Shall sum my count and make my old excuse,'
Proving his beauty by succession thine.
  This were to be new made when thou art old,
  And see thy blood warm when thou feel'st it cold.

3 *proud livery*] uniform of which you are proud 4 *weed*] piece of clothing 8 *thriftless praise*] unprofitable form of praise 9 How much more would putting your beauty to use deserve praise 11 *sum my count*] make up the balance of my account; *make my old excuse*] make justification for me in my old age

3

Look in thy glass, and tell the face thou viewest
Now is the time that face should form another,
Whose fresh repair if now thou now renewest,
Thou dost beguile the world, unbless some mother.
For where is she so fair whose unear'd womb
Disdains the tillage of thy husbandry?
Or who is he so fond, will be the tomb
Of his self-love to stop posterity?
Thou art thy mother's glass, and she in thee
Calls back the lovely April of her prime:
So thou through windows of thine age shalt see,
Despite of wrinkles, this thy golden time.
    But if thou live remember'd not to be,
    Die single, and thine image dies with thee.

1 *glass*] mirror 3 *repair*] condition 4 *beguile*] cheat; *unbless some mother*] frustrate someone of motherhood 5 *unear'd*] unploughed 6 *tillage of thy husbandry*] cultivation by you as husband, farmer 7 *fond*] foolish 9 *glass*] mirror 11 *windows of thine age*] your eyes in age 13 *remember'd not to be*] to be forgotten

5

Those hours that with gentle work did frame
The lovely gaze where every eye doth dwell
Will play the tyrants to the very same,
And that unfair which fairly doth excel:
For never-resting time leads summer on
To hideous winter, and confounds him there,
Sap check'd with frost, and lusty leaves quite gone,
Beauty o'er-snow'd, and bareness everywhere.
Then were not summer's distillation left,
A liquid prisoner pent in walls of glass,
Beauty's effect with beauty were bereft –
Nor it, nor no remembrance what it was.
But flowers distill'd, though they with winter meet,
Leese but their show; their substance still lives sweet.

4 *that unfair which fairly*] make that ugly which in its beauty 6 *confounds*] destroys 9 *summer's distillation*] summer's essence, its perfume 11 *were bereft*] would be taken away 12 Neither beauty nor memory of what beauty was would be left 14 *Leese*] lose

8

Music to hear, why hear'st thou music sadly?
Sweets with sweets war not, joy delights in joy;
Why lov'st thou that which thou receiv'st not gladly,
Or else receiv'st with pleasure thine annoy?
If the true concord of well-tuned sounds,
By unions married, do offend thine ear,
They do but sweetly chide thee, who confounds
In singleness the parts that thou shouldst bear.
Mark how one string, sweet husband to another,
Strikes each in each by mutual ordering,
Resembling sire and child and happy mother,
Who, all in one, one pleasing note do sing;
    Whose speechless song, being many, seeming one,
    Sings this to thee: 'Thou single wilt prove none.'

1 *Music to hear*] You who are music to hear   5 *concord*] harmony   6 *By unions married*] brought together in satisfying matches   8 *singleness*] unmarried state; *parts*] diverse musical lines, different roles (husband, father) to be played   10 *Strikes . . . ordering*] (Probably alludes to the double-strung lute in which two strings, tuned sympathetically, sound the same note)   14 *Thou single wilt prove none*] cf. the proverb 'One is no number'

9

Is it for fear to wet a widow's eye
That thou consum'st thyself in single life?
Ah! if thou issueless shalt hap to die,
The world will wail thee like a makeless wife.
The world will be thy widow, and still weep
That thou no form of thee hast left behind,
When every private widow well may keep
By children's eyes her husband's shape in mind.
Look, what an unthrift in the world doth spend
Shifts but his place, for still the world enjoys it;
But beauty's waste hath in the world an end,
And kept unus'd, the user so destroys it.
    No love toward others in that bosom sits
    That on himself such murd'rous shame commits.

1 *wet a widow's eye*] make a widow weep 3 *issueless*] childless 4 *wail*] mourn for; *makeless*] without a mate 6 *form*] likeness 7 *private*] separate 8 *By*] by means of 9 *unthrift*] prodigal 10 *his*] its 11 *beauty's waste*] beauty wasted like the prodigal's money

12

When I do count the clock that tells the time,
And see the brave day sunk in hideous night;
When I behold the violet past prime,
And sable curls all silver'd o'er with white;
When lofty trees I see barren of leaves,
Which erst from heat did canopy the herd,
And summer's green all girded up in sheaves
Borne on the bier with white and bristly beard:
Then of thy beauty do I question make,
That thou among the wastes of time must go,
Since sweets and beauties do themselves forsake,
And die as fast as they see others grow;
    And nothing 'gainst Time's scythe can make defence
    Save breed, to brave him when he takes thee hence.

6 *erst*] formerly 8 *bier*] barrow 9 *of thy beauty do I question make*] I ponder your beauty questioningly 10 *among the wastes of time*] where Time's waste things go 11 *themselves forsake*] change in their nature 14 *Save breed, to brave him*] except children, to defy Time

15

When I consider every thing that grows
Holds in perfection but a little moment,
That this huge stage presenteth naught but shows
Whereon the stars in secret influence comment;
When I perceive that men as plants increase,
Cheered and check'd even by the selfsame sky,
Vaunt in their youthful sap, at height decrease,
And wear their brave state out of memory:
Then the conceit of this inconstant stay
Sets you most rich in youth before my sight,
Where wasteful Time debateth with Decay
To change your day of youth to sullied night;
    And all in war with Time for love of you,
    As he takes from you, I engraft you new.

4 *in secret influence comment*] exercise an inscrutable influence according to their judgment 6 *Cheered and check'd*] encouraged and restrained 7 *Vaunt*] exult 8 *wear . . . memory*] wear their finery until it is worn out and forgotten 9 *conceit*] thought 11 *debateth*] contests 13 *all in war*] utterly at war 14 *engraft you new*] give you new life (by writing about you)

16

But wherefore do not you a mightier way
Make war upon this bloody tyrant, Time,
And fortify yourself in your decay
With means more blessed than my barren rhyme?
Now stand you on the top of happy hours,
And many maiden gardens yet unset
With virtuous wish would bear your living flowers,
Much liker than your painted counterfeit.
So should the lines of life that life repair
Which this time's pencil or my pupil pen
Neither in inward worth nor outward fair
Can make you live yourself in eyes of men.
    To give away yourself keeps yourself still;
    And you must live, drawn by your own sweet skill.

1 *mightier*] more powerful (than through my verses about you) 3 *fortify*] strengthen 6 *unset*] unplanted 8 *liker*] more like you; *counterfeit*] portrait 9 *the lines of life*] the line which, by having children, the young man would continue 10 *this time's pencil*] the brush of today's artist 11 *fair*] beauty 13 *give away yourself*] i.e. in marriage or in your children

17

Who will believe my verse in time to come,
If it were fill'd with your most high deserts?
– Though yet, heaven knows, it is but as a tomb
Which hides your life, and shows not half your parts.
If I could write the beauty of your eyes
And in fresh numbers number all your graces,
The age to come would say 'This poet lies;
Such heavenly touches ne'er touch'd earthly faces.'
So should my papers, yellow'd with their age,
Be scorn'd, like old men of less truth than tongue,
And your true rights be term'd a poet's rage
And stretched metre of an antique song.
    But were some child of yours alive that time,
    You should live twice: in it, and in my rhyme.

6 *numbers*] verses 12 *your true rights*] your due in all truth; *a poet's rage*] the product of poetic hyperbole 12 *stretched metre*] exaggerated measure; *antique*] (pronounced 'antic') ancient

18

Shall I compare thee to a summer's day?
Thou art more lovely and more temperate.
Rough winds do shake the darling buds of May,
And summer's lease hath all too short a date;
Sometime too hot the eye of heaven shines,
And often is his gold complexion dimm'd,
And every fair from fair sometime declines,
By chance or nature's changing course untrimm'd;
But thy eternal summer shall not fade
Nor lose possession of that fair thou ow'st,
Nor shall death brag thou wander'st in his shade,
When in eternal lines to time thou grow'st.
So long as men can breathe or eyes can see,
So long lives this, and this gives life to thee.

4 *date*] time allotted to it 7 *fair from fair*] beautiful thing from beauty 8 *untrimm'd*] stripped of ornament 10 *fair thou ow'st*] beauty you own 12 *lines*] verse, and possibly lines of descent; *to time thou grow'st*] you reach as far as time will go 14 *this*] this sonnet, and possibly the truth it conveys

19

Devouring Time, blunt thou the lion's paws,
And make the earth devour her own sweet brood;
Pluck the keen teeth from the fierce tiger's jaws,
And burn the long-liv'd phoenix in her blood;
Make glad and sorry seasons as thou fleet'st,
And do whate'er thou wilt, swift-footed Time,
To the wide world and all her fading sweets;
But I forbid thee one most heinous crime.
O, carve not with thy hours my love's fair brow,
Nor draw no lines there with thine antique pen.
Him in thy course untainted do allow
For beauty's pattern to succeeding men.
    Yet do thy worst, old Time; despite thy wrong,
    My love shall in my verse ever live young.

4 *phoenix*] bird supposed to be consumed periodically in flames and then to revive. There was only one phoenix in the world 10 *antique*] (pronounced 'antic') ancient 11 *untainted*] untouched, unsullied

20

A woman's face with Nature's own hand painted
Hast thou, the master-mistress of my passion;
A woman's gentle heart, but not acquainted
With shifting change as is false women's fashion;
An eye more bright than theirs, less false in rolling,
Gilding the object whereupon it gazeth;
A man in hue, all hues in his controlling,
Which steals men's eyes and women's souls amazeth.
And for a woman wert thou first created,
Till Nature as she wrought thee fell a-doting,
And by addition me of thee defeated
By adding one thing to my purpose nothing.
    But since she prick'd thee out for women's pleasure,
    Mine be thy love, and thy love's use their treasure.

1 *with Nature's own hand painted*] i.e. naturally not cosmetically beautiful 5 *rolling*] passing from one to another 6 *Gilding*] adding lustre to 7 *A man in hue*] a man in appearance, a fine man; *all hues in his controlling*] to whom all others are subject, or which may command every aspect of human form (e.g. both male and female) 10 *fell a-doting*] became besotted 11 *addition*] adding something (a penis) 13 *prick'd*] marked (with a quibble, as in 'thing' in the previous line)

21

So is it not with me as with that Muse
Stirr'd by a painted beauty to his verse,
Who heaven itself for ornament doth use,
And every fair with his fair doth rehearse,
Making a couplement of proud compare
With sun and moon, with earth and sea's rich gems,
With April's first-born flowers, and all things rare
That heaven's air in this huge rondure hems.
O let me, true in love, but truly write,
And then believe me, my love is as fair
As any mother's child, though not so bright
As those gold candles fix'd in heaven's air.
    Let them say more that like of hearsay well;
    I will not praise, that purpose not to sell.

1 *Muse*] poet 2 *Stirr'd*] who is inspired; *painted*] i.e. artificially derived 4 *fair with his fair*] beautiful thing with his beauty; *rehearse*] join together in his words 5 *Making a couplement of proud compare*] linking the subject of his praise in fine comparison 8 *rondure*] round of the world or universe 9 *but truly*] only with truth 13 *hearsay*] empty talk

23

As an unperfect actor on the stage,
Who with his fear is put besides his part,
Or some fierce thing replete with too much rage,
Whose strength's abundance weakens his own heart,
So I, for fear of trust, forget to say
The perfect ceremony of love's rite,
And in mine own love's strength seem to decay,
O'er-charg'd with burden of mine own love's might.
O let my books be then the eloquence
And dumb presagers of my speaking breast,
Who plead for love, and look for recompense
More than that tongue that more hath more express'd.
O, learn to read what silent love hath writ;
To hear with eyes belongs to love's fine wit.

1 *unperfect*] ill-prepared 5 *for fear of trust*] because I lack trust (in myself or, possibly, you) 6 *rite*] ritual, but also right 7 *decay*] weaken, falter 9 *books*] writings (probably these poems) 10 *presagers*] heralds; *speaking*] (though silent) 12 *more hath more*] has more often or more finely, more copiously

25

Let those who are in favour with their stars
Of public honour and proud titles boast,
Whilst I, whom fortune of such triumph bars,
Unlook'd-for joy in that I honour most.
Great princes' favourites their fair leaves spread
But as the marigold at the sun's eye,
And in themselves their pride lies buried,
For at a frown they in their glory die.
The painful warrior famoused for might,
After a thousand victories once foil'd
Is from the book of honour razed quite,
And all the rest forgot for which he toil'd.
Then happy I, that love and am belov'd
Where I may not remove nor be remov'd.

4 *Unlook'd-for*] unregarded, and against expectation; *joy in that*] delight in the person, or in the fact that 6 *marigold*] flower which opens and shuts depending on the sun's intensity 9 *painful*] both causing and suffering pain; *famoused*] renowned 11 *razed*] erased 14 *remove*] change affection; *be remov'd*] (from favour)

27

Weary with toil I haste me to my bed,
The dear repose for limbs with travel tir'd;
But then begins a journey in my head
To work my mind when body's work's expir'd;
For then my thoughts, from far where I abide,
Intend a zealous pilgrimage to thee,
And keep my drooping eyelids open wide,
Looking on darkness which the blind do see:
Save that my soul's imaginary sight
Presents thy shadow to my sightless view,
Which like a jewel hung in ghastly night
Makes black night beauteous and her old face new.
    Lo, thus by day my limbs, by night my mind,
    For thee, and for myself, no quiet find.

2 *travel*] journeying, and work 4 *expir'd*] concluded at the end of day, and in sleep 6 *Intend*] go on 9 *imaginary*] imaginative, imaging 10 *shadow*] image; *sightless view*] unseeing vision

29

When, in disgrace with Fortune and men's eyes,
I all alone beweep my outcast state,
And trouble deaf heaven with my bootless cries,
And look upon myself and curse my fate,
Wishing me like to one more rich in hope,
Featur'd like him, like him with friends possess'd,
Desiring this man's art and that man's scope,
With what I most enjoy contented least:
Yet in these thoughts myself almost despising,
Haply I think on thee, and then my state,
Like to the lark at break of day arising,
From sullen earth sings hymns at heaven's gate;
    For thy sweet love remember'd such wealth brings
    That then I scorn to change my state with kings.

1 *in disgrace*] out of favour 3 *bootless*] pointless 7 *art*] skill; *scope*] range 8 *most enjoy*] have most of, and take most pleasure in 10 *Haply*] by chance 12 *From sullen earth*] Leaving dark and heavy earth (my discontent)

30

When to the sessions of sweet silent thought
I summon up remembrance of things past,
I sigh the lack of many a thing I sought,
And with old woes new wail my dear time's waste.
Then can I drown an eye, unus'd to flow,
For precious friends hid in death's dateless night,
And weep afresh love's long since cancell'd woe,
And moan th'expense of many a vanish'd sight.
Then can I grieve at grievances foregone,
And heavily from woe to woe tell o'er
The sad account of fore-bemoaned moan,
Which I new pay as if not paid before.
    But if the while I think on thee, dear friend,
    All losses are restor'd, and sorrows end.

1 *sessions*] court sittings (cf. 'summon up' in next line) 3 *sigh*] sigh for 4 *new wail my dear time's waste*] lament once more how my precious time has been wasted, or laid waste (by the death of friends) 5 *flow*] i.e. in tears 6 *dateless*] unending 7 *cancell'd*] paid off 8 *expense of many a vanish'd sight*] passing of many a thing seen, expenditure of many a sigh in the past 9 *foregone*] that are past or given over 10 *heavily*] sadly 11 *fore-bemoaned moan*] laments already once or more lamented

31

Thy bosom is endeared with all hearts
Which I by lacking have supposed dead;
And there reigns love, and all love's loving parts,
And all those friends which I thought buried.
How many a holy and obsequious tear
Hath dear religious love stol'n from mine eye
As interest of the dead, which now appear
But things remov'd that hidden in thee lie!
Thou art the grave where buried love doth live,
Hung with the trophies of my lovers gone,
Who all their parts of me to thee did give:
That due of many now is thine alone.
    Their images I lov'd I view in thee,
    And thou, all they, hast all the all of me.

1 *endeared with*] made more precious by 2 *lacking*] not having (because they are dead (cf. the previous sonnet)) 5 *obsequious*] funereal 7 *interest of*] what is due to 9 *buried*] (two syllables) 11 *parts of me*] shares in me 12 *That due of many*] what was owed to many (my love) 13 *Their images I loved*] the images of those whom I loved

33

Full many a glorious morning have I seen
Flatter the mountain tops with sovereign eye,
Kissing with golden face the meadows green,
Gilding pale streams with heavenly alchemy,
Anon permit the basest clouds to ride
With ugly rack on his celestial face,
And from the forlorn world his visage hide,
Stealing unseen to west with this disgrace.
Even so my sun one early morn did shine
With all triumphant splendour on my brow,
But out, alack, he was but one hour mine;
The region cloud hath mask'd him from me now.
    Yet him for this my love no whit disdaineth;
    Suns of the world may stain when heaven's sun staineth.

2 *Flatter*] dignify beyond their due; *sovereign eye*] royal countenance (of the sun) 4 *Gilding*] turning to gold 6 *rack*] driving clouds 7 *forlorn*] (accented on the first syllable) 12 *region*] belonging to the upper air 13 *no whit*] not at all 14 *stain*] lose lustre

34

Why didst thou promise such a beauteous day
And make me travel forth without my cloak,
To let base clouds o'ertake me in my way,
Hiding thy brav'ry in their rotten smoke?
'Tis not enough that through the cloud thou break
To dry the rain on my storm-beaten face,
For no man well of such a salve can speak
That heals the wound and cures not the disgrace:
Nor can thy shame give physic to my grief;
Though thou repent, yet I have still the loss.
Th' offender's sorrow lends but weak relief
To him that bears the strong offence's cross.
Ah, but those tears are pearl which thy love sheds,
And they are rich, and ransom all ill deeds.

3 *base*] dark 4 *brav'ry*] finery; *rotten smoke*] unwholesome breath 7 *salve*] palliative or remedy 9 *thy shame give physic to*] your being ashamed be a medicine for 12 *bears the . . . cross*] suffers the pain 14 *ransom*] make up for

35

No more be griev'd at that which thou hast done:
Roses have thorns, and silver fountains mud,
Clouds and eclipses stain both moon and sun,
And loathsome canker lives in sweetest bud.
All men make faults, and even I in this,
Authorizing thy trespass with compare,
Myself corrupting, salving thy amiss,
Excusing thy sins more than thy sins are;
For to thy sensual fault I bring in sense –
Thy adverse party is thy advocate –
And 'gainst myself a lawful plea commence,
Such civil war is in my love and hate,
    That I an accessory needs must be
    To that sweet thief which sourly robs from me.

3 *stain*] darken 4 *canker*] destructive worm, grub, etc. 6 Justifying your wrongdoing by comparisons (*authorizing* is accented on the second syllable) 7 *salving*] making good; *amiss*] offence 8 Producing excuses for more (or worse) sins than those you have actually committed 9 *bring in sense*] bring intellect to help 10 The person opposing you speaks on your behalf 11 *commence*] (the proper term for beginning an action in law) 14 *sourly*] with bitter effect

36

Let me confess that we two must be twain,
Although our undivided loves are one;
So shall those blots that do with me remain,
Without thy help by me be borne alone.
In our two loves there is but one respect,
Though in our lives a separable spite,
Which, though it alter not love's sole effect,
Yet doth it steal sweet hours from love's delight.
I may not evermore acknowledge thee,
Lest my bewailed guilt should do thee shame,
Nor thou with public kindness honour me
Unless thou take that honour from thy name.
    But do not so. I love thee in such sort
    As, thou being mine, mine is thy good report.

1 *be twain*] be parted, be separated one from another 3 *those blots*] defects inherent in me or acquired as a result of your conduct (cf. preceding sonnets) 5 *one respect*] one thing that matters 6 *separable spite*] pain of separation 9 *not evermore*] nevermore 10 *bewailed*] lamented 12 Without diminishing the honour due to your rank (*name* is both personal and family reputation) 13–14] (These lines also conclude Sonnet 96) 14 *report*] reputation

40

Take all my loves, my love, yea, take them all:
What hast thou then more than thou hadst before?
No love, my love, that thou mayst true love call;
All mine was thine before thou hadst this more.
Then if for my love thou my love receivest,
I cannot blame thee for my love thou usest;
But yet be blam'd if thou thyself deceivest
By wilful taste of what thyself refusest.
I do forgive thy robb'ry, gentle thief,
Although thou steal thee all my poverty;
And yet, love knows it is a greater grief
To bear love's wrong than hate's known injury.
  Lascivious grace, in whom all ill well shows,
  Kill me with spites; yet we must not be foes.

1 *my loves*] the people I love or who love me, and the love I bear them or they bear me 3 (You had my *true love* before you took my other loves from me) 5 If out of affection for me you entertain the person I love (the lady of Sonnets 127–52?) 6 *for my love thou usest*] because you take advantage of my love, and the person I love 8 *wilful taste*] perverse sampling; *thyself*] i.e. your better self 10 *all my poverty*] all that I have in my poverty 13 *Lascivious grace*] wanton beauty (the phrase implies a mixture of admiration and impatient disapproval) 14 *spites*] injuries

41

Those pretty wrongs that liberty commits,
When I am sometime absent from thy heart,
Thy beauty and thy years full well befits,
For still temptation follows where thou art.
Gentle thou art, and therefore to be won,
Beauteous thou art, therefore to be assail'd;
And when a woman woos, what woman's son
Will sourly leave her till she have prevail'd?
Ay me! but yet thou mightst my seat forbear,
And chide thy beauty and thy straying youth,
Who lead thee in their riot even there
Where thou art forc'd to break a two-fold troth:
    Hers, by thy beauty tempting her to thee,
    Thine, by thy beauty being false to me.

1 *pretty*] delightful, trivial (with some irony); *liberty*] freedom which may or may not be licentious 3 *befits*] singular verb for plural subject (*wrongs*) 4 *still*] continually 5 *Gentle*] without coarseness, of good birth 9 *my seat forbear*] decline to take my place 11 *riot*] prodigal conduct

43

When most I wink, then do mine eyes best see,
For all the day they view things unrespected;
But when I sleep, in dreams they look on thee,
And, darkly bright, are bright in dark directed.
Then thou, whose shadow shadows doth make bright,
How would thy shadow's form form happy show
To the clear day with thy much clearer light,
When to unseeing eyes thy shade shines so!
How would, I say, mine eyes be blessed made
By looking on thee in the living day,
When in dead night thy fair imperfect shade
Through heavy sleep on sightless eyes doth stay!
    All days are nights to see till I see thee,
    And nights bright days when dreams do show thee me.

2 *unrespected*] not regarded 4 And, blindly seeing, are by their illumination in the dark given direction and purpose 5 *shadow shadows doth make bright*] image brings light to darkness 6 *thy shadow's form*] the substance underlying your image 7 *clear*] bright 8 *unseeing*] i.e. closed in sleep 11 *imperfect*] because only an image

53

What is your substance, whereof are you made,
That millions of strange shadows on you tend?
Since everyone hath, every one, one shade,
And you, but one, can every shadow lend.
Describe Adonis, and the counterfeit
Is poorly imitated after you;
On Helen's cheek all art of beauty set,
And you in Grecian tires are painted new.
Speak of the spring and foison of the year:
The one doth shadow of your beauty show,
The other as your bounty doth appear;
And you in every blessed shape we know.
    In all external grace you have some part,
    But you like none, none you, for constant heart.

2 *strange shadows*] likenesses of other people; *tend*] wait like servants or court followers 4 And in you, though you are only one person, every attribute of others can be found 5 *counterfeit*] description, inauthentic in comparison with you 8 *tires*] dress 9 *foison*] harvest

54

O, how much more doth beauty beauteous seem
By that sweet ornament which truth doth give!
The rose looks fair, but fairer we it deem
For that sweet odour which doth in it live.
The canker blooms have full as deep a dye
As the perfum'd tincture of the roses –
Hang on such thorns, and play as wantonly
When summer's breath their masked buds discloses;
But for their virtue only is their show
They live unwoo'd and unrespected fade –
Die to themselves. Sweet roses do not so;
Of their sweet deaths are sweetest odours made:
    And so of you, beauteous and lovely youth,
    When that shall vade, by verse distils your truth.

2 *truth*] integrity, constancy 5 *canker blooms*] dog roses, which have no perfume; *deep a dye*] rich a colour 6 *tincture*] colouring 7 *such*] similar; *play*] wave; *wantonly*] freely 8 *masked*] concealed (in the bud, which opens to the summer breeze) 9 But because their only goodness is in their appearance 10 *unrespected*] unregarded 11 *to themselves*] unregarded 12 (Perfume is made from roses) 14 When your beauty goes, or fades, your truth will distil into its essence by means of my verse

55

Not marble nor the gilded monuments
Of princes shall outlive this powerful rhyme,
But you shall shine more bright in these contents
Than unswept stone besmear'd with sluttish time.
When wasteful war shall statues overturn
And broils root out the work of masonry,
Nor Mars his sword nor war's quick fire shall burn
The living record of your memory.
'Gainst death and all oblivious enmity
Shall you pace forth; your praise shall still find room
Even in the eyes of all posterity
That wear this world out to the ending doom.
    So, till the judgement that yourself arise,
    You live in this, and dwell in lovers' eyes.

3 *these contents*] (stressed on the second syllable) what is contained in this *rhyme* 4 *stone*] funerary monument, or memorial stone set in a church floor; *with sluttish time*] in the course of, as a result of, time's slovenly passage 6 *broils*] battles, skirmishes 7 *Mars his sword*] the sword of Mars, Roman god of war; *quick*] vigorous, vital 9 *oblivious enmity*] forgetfulness hostile to your memory 12 That survive with this world to the doomsday that ends it 13 *judgement that yourself*] Day of Judgement when you

56

Sweet love, renew thy force; be it not said
Thy edge should blunter be than appetite,
Which but today by feeding is allay'd,
Tomorrow sharpen'd in his former might.
So, love, be thou; although today thou fill
Thy hungry eyes even till they wink with fullness,
Tomorrow see again, and do not kill
The spirit of love with a perpetual dullness.
Let this sad interim like the ocean be
Which parts the shore, where two contracted new
Come daily to the banks, that when they see
Return of love, more bless'd may be the view.
  Or call it winter, which, being full of care,
  Makes summer's welcome thrice more wish'd, more rare.

1 *love*] (the emotion) 2 *should blunter be*] is blunter; *appetite*] hunger, lust 6 *wink with fullness*] drop with being sated 9 *in terim*] (two syllables: *Intrim* in 1609) temporary state of affairs 10 *contracted new*] newly contracted lovers 14 *wish'd*] wished for

57

Being your slave, what should I do but tend
Upon the hours and times of your desire?
I have no precious time at all to spend,
Nor services to do, till you require.
Nor dare I chide the world-without-end hour
Whilst I, my sovereign, watch the clock for you,
Nor think the bitterness of absence sour
When you have bid your servant once adieu;
Nor dare I question with my jealous thought
Where you may be, or your affairs suppose,
But, like a sad slave, stay and think of naught
Save, where you are, how happy you make those.
    So true a fool is love that in your will,
    Though you do anything, he thinks no ill.

1 *tend*] wait 2 *of your desire*] when you want something (of me) 4 *require*] command, ask 5 *world-without-end hour*] hour which seems to have no end 9 *jealous*] which is or which might be mistrustful 10 *your affairs suppose*] guess at the business that occupies you 12 Except how happy you make the people who are with you 13 *will*] desire (capable of a bad sense), also possibly Will (Shakespeare)

58

That god forbid, that made me first your slave,
I should in thought control your times of pleasure,
Or at your hand th'account of hours to crave,
Being your vassal bound to stay your leisure.
O, let me suffer, being at your beck,
Th'imprison'd absence of your liberty,
And patience, tame to sufferance, bide each check,
Without accusing you of injury.
Be where you list, your charter is so strong
That you yourself may privilege your time
To what you will; to you it doth belong
Yourself to pardon of self-doing crime.
  I am to wait, though waiting so be hell,
  Not blame your pleasure, be it ill or well.

1 *That god*] i.e. Love 2 *control*] call to account 4 *stay*] await 6 *imprison'd*] like a prison for me; *of your liberty*] created by your freedom (with a hint of a bad sense – 'excessive freedom') 7 *tame to sufferance*] meekly putting up with what has to be endured; *bide each check*] put up with every snub 9 *charter*] document giving right to act as judge and to grant rights to others 10 *privilege*] authorize 12 *of self-doing crime*] for a crime you have yourself committed 13 *I am*] I am expected 14 *be it ill or well*] whether what pleases you (possibly a sexual meaning here), or my blaming it, is a good or bad thing

59

If there be nothing new, but that which is
Hath been before, how are our brains beguil'd,
Which, labouring for invention, bear amiss
The second burden of a former child!
O, that record could with a backward look,
Even of five hundred courses of the sun,
Show me your image in some antique book
Since mind at first in character was done,
That I might see what the old world could say
To this composed wonder of your frame;
Whether we are mended or whe'er better they,
Or whether revolution be the same.
O sure I am, the wits of former days
To subjects worse have given admiring praise.

2 *beguil'd*] misled 3–4 Which, labouring to find a theme or topic, mistakenly give birth to a child that has been born once already, i.e. which strive for originality and are bound not to find it 5 *record*] (stressed on the second syllable) memory, history 6 *courses of the sun*] years 7 *antique*] (pronounced '*antic*') old 8 Since thoughts were first set down in writing 10 *composed wonder of your frame*] harmonious miracle of your form 11 *mended*] improved 12 *revolution be the same*] cycles of time produce no change 13 *wits*] men of gift

60

Like as the waves make towards the pebbled shore,
So do our minutes hasten to their end;
Each changing place with that which goes before,
In sequent toil all forwards do contend.
Nativity, once in the main of light,
Crawls to maturity, wherewith being crown'd
Crooked eclipses 'gainst his glory fight,
And Time that gave doth now his gift confound.
Time doth transfix the flourish set on youth
And delves the parallels in beauty's brow,
Feeds on the rarities of nature's truth,
And nothing stands but for his scythe to mow.
And yet to times in hope my verse shall stand,
Praising thy worth despite his cruel hand.

4 *In sequent toil*] labouring one after another; *contend*] strive 5 *Na tivity*] the new-born child; *main*] ocean (of light – the world) 7 *Crooked*] malignant (the image is astrological) 8 *confound*] destroy 9 *trans-fix*] impale, as on a weapon; *flourish*] embellishment, sign of health10 *delves the parallels*] digs the lines 11 *rarities of nature's truth*] finest things of nature's perfection 13 *times in hope*] times only dreamt of as yet

61

Is it thy will thy image should keep open
My heavy eyelids to the weary night?
Dost thou desire my slumbers should be broken,
While shadows like to thee do mock my sight?
Is it thy spirit that thou send'st from thee
So far from home into my deeds to pry,
To find out shames and idle hours in me,
The scope and tenor of thy jealousy?
O, no, thy love, though much, is not so great;
It is my love that keeps mine eye awake,
Mine own true love that doth my rest defeat,
To play the watchman ever for thy sake.
 For thee watch I, whilst thou dost wake elsewhere,
 From me far off, with others all too near.

2 *weary night*] night in which (of which?) men are weary 8 *scope and tenor*] focus and chief concern (probably applied to *shames and idle hours*) 12 *ever*] continually 13 *watch*] look out anxiously, and stay awake

62

Sin of self-love possesseth all mine eye,
And all my soul, and all my every part;
And for this sin there is no remedy,
It is so grounded inward in my heart.
Methinks no face so gracious is as mine,
No shape so true, no truth of such account;
And for myself mine own worth do define
As I all other in all worths surmount.
But when my glass shows me myself indeed,
Beated and chopp'd with tann'd antiquity,
Mine own self-love quite contrary I read –
Self so self-loving were iniquity.
  'Tis thee, my self, that for myself I praise,
  Painting my age with beauty of thy days.

4 *inward*] i.e. deeply 6 *truth*] constancy 8 *As*] as if; *other*] others 9 *glass*] mirror; *indeed*] as I really am 10 My skin tanned by age, wind-beaten and cracked 11 *quite contrary I read*] I interpret quite differently 12 It would be wicked for one to love oneself in such a way 13 *for myself*] in my place 14 Making my aged self beautiful with the attributes of your youth

63

Against my love shall be as I am now,
With Time's injurious hand crush'd and o'erworn;
When hours have drain'd his blood and fill'd his brow
With lines and wrinkles; when his youthful morn
Hath travell'd on to age's steepy night,
And all those beauties whereof now he's king
Are vanishing, or vanish'd out of sight,
Stealing away the treasure of his spring:
For such a time do I now fortify
Against confounding age's cruel knife,
That he shall never cut from memory
My sweet love's beauty, though my lover's life.
  His beauty shall in these black lines be seen,
  And they shall live, and he in them still green.

1 *Against*] in preparation for the time when 2 *o'erworn*] worn out 5 *steepy*] fast declining 9 *fortify*] build defences 10 *confounding*] destructive 11–13 (The young man's life will not survive, but his beauty will, preserved in these verses) 14 *still green*] for ever flourishing

64

When I have seen by Time's fell hand defac'd
The rich proud cost of outworn buried age;
When sometime-lofty towers I see down raz'd,
And brass eternal slave to mortal rage;
When I have seen the hungry ocean gain
Advantage on the kingdom of the shore,
And the firm soil win of the wat'ry main,
Increasing store with loss and loss with store;
When I have seen such interchange of state,
Or state itself confounded to decay,
Ruin hath taught me thus to ruminate,
That Time will come and take my love away.
    This thought is as a death, which cannot choose
    But weep to have that which it fears to lose.

1 *fell*] cruel 2 *cost*] things gained at high cost; *outworn*] worn out, old-fashioned; *buried*] (two syllables) i.e. in the past 4 *brass eternal*] everlasting brass; *mortal rage*] death's fury 7 *main*] ocean 8 Each gaining as it loses and losing as it gains 9 *interchange of state*] exchange of condition 10 *state*] i.e. prosperous state

65

Since brass, nor stone, nor earth, nor boundless sea,
But sad mortality o'ersways their power,
How with this rage shall beauty hold a plea,
Whose action is no stronger than a flower?
O, how shall summer's honey breath hold out
Against the wrackful siege of batt'ring days
When rocks impregnable are not so stout,
Nor gates of steel so strong, but Time decays?
O fearful meditation! Where, alack,
Shall Time's best jewel from Time's chest lie hid,
Or what strong hand can hold his swift foot back,
Or who his spoil of beauty can forbid?
    O, none, unless this miracle have might,
    That in black ink my love may still shine bright.

1 *Since*] since there is neither 2 *o'ersways*] overrules 3 *hold a plea*] uphold a suit 4 *action*] case at law 6 *wrackful*] destructive; *batt'ring days*] (like battering rams) 8 *decays*] makes decay 12 *spoil*] ruination

66

Tir'd with all these, for restful death I cry,
As, to behold desert a beggar born,
And needy nothing trimm'd in jollity,
And purest faith unhappily forsworn,
And gilded honour shamefully misplac'd,
And maiden virtue rudely strumpeted,
And right perfection wrongfully disgrac'd,
And strength by limping sway disabled,
And art made tongue-tied by authority,
And folly, doctor-like, controlling skill,
And simple truth miscall'd simplicity,
And captive good attending captain ill:
　　Tir'd with all these, from these would I be gone,
　　Save that to die I leave my love alone.

2 *As*] as for instance; *desert*] merit 3 *nothing*] worthlessness; *trimm'd in jollity*] dressed up to celebrate 4 *forsworn*] abandoned 5 *gilded*] golden; *shamefully misplac'd*] awarded to the undeserving in shameful manner 6 *strumpeted*] prostituted 8 *limping sway*] halting authority; *disabled*] (four syllables: 'disable-èd') 9 *art*] learning 10 *controlling*] supervising, curbing 14 *to die*] by dying

67

Ah, wherefore with infection should he live
And with his presence grace impiety,
That sin by him advantage should achieve
And lace itself with his society?
Why should false painting imitate his cheek
And steal dead seeming of his living hue?
Why should poor beauty indirectly seek
Roses of shadow, since his rose is true?
Why should he live now Nature bankrupt is,
Beggar'd of blood to blush through lively veins?
For she hath no exchequer now but his,
And 'prov'd of many, lives upon his gains?
    O, him she stores to show what wealth she had
    In days long since, before these last so bad.

1 *with infection*] where infection is 4 *lace*] adorn 5 *false painting*] cosmetics 6 *dead seeming of*] lifeless appearance from 7 *indirectly seek*] deviously seek to realize itself in 8 *Roses of shadow*] illusory beauty (rosy cheeks produced by cosmetics) 9 *bankrupt*] (because she has given all her wealth to the young man) 11 *exchequer*] treasury 12 *'prov'd*] approved (*proud* in 1609): *his gains*] what he has gained (from her)

68

Thus is his cheek the map of days outworn,
When beauty liv'd and died as flowers do now,
Before these bastard signs of fair were borne
Or durst inhabit on a living brow;
Before the golden tresses of the dead,
The right of sepulchres, were shorn away
To live a second life on second head;
Ere beauty's dead fleece made another gay.
In him those holy antique hours are seen
Without all ornament, itself and true,
Making no summer of another's green,
Robbing no old to dress his beauty new;
  And him as for a map doth Nature store,
  To show false Art what beauty was of yore.

1 *outworn*] gone by, worn out of fashion 3 *bastard signs of fair*] low and illegitimate marks of beauty (e.g. the cosmetics of Sonnet 67) 4 *durst inhabit*] (implies assumption of a right when opposed to the passive sense of *were borne*) 6 *The right of sepulchres*] which should have been buried with them 7 *a second life*] (as a wig) 8 *Ere beauty's dead fleece*] before the hair of a dead beauty 9 *antique*] (pronounced 'antic') ancient 11 *of*] out of 13 *store*] keep 14 *false Art*] art that deceives (by use of cosmetics etc.)

69

Those parts of thee that the world's eye doth view
Want nothing that the thought of hearts can mend.
All tongues, the voice of souls, give thee that due,
Utt'ring bare truth even so as foes commend.
Thy outward thus with outward praise is crown'd,
But those same tongues, that give thee so thine own,
In other accents do this praise confound
By seeing farther than the eye hath shown.
They look into the beauty of thy mind,
And that in guess they measure by thy deeds.
Then, churls, their thoughts – although their eyes were kind –
To thy fair flower add the rank smell of weeds:
    But why thy odour matcheth not thy show,
    The soil is this, that thou dost common grow.

2 *Want*] lack 4 *bare*] simple; *even so as*] so that even 6 *thine own*] what is due to you 7 *accents*] tones; *confound*] destroy 12 *thy fair flower*] i.e. your beauty 14 *soil*] reason (why the flower is not matched in beauty by its perfume), stain; *common*] vulgar, cheap, indiscriminate

71

No longer mourn for me when I am dead
Than you shall hear the surly sullen bell
Give warning to the world that I am fled
From this vile world, with vilest worms to dwell.
Nay, if you read this line, remember not
The hand that writ it; for I love you so
That I in your sweet thoughts would be forgot
If thinking on me then should make you woe.
O, if, I say, you look upon this verse
When I perhaps compounded am with clay,
Do not so much as my poor name rehearse,
But let your love even with my life decay,
    Lest the wise world should look into your moan,
    And mock you with me after I am gone.

8 *make*] cause   11 *rehearse*] say over   13 *moan*] sorrow

72

O, lest the world should task you to recite
What merit liv'd in me that you should love,
After my death, dear love, forget me quite;
For you in me can nothing worthy prove,
Unless you would devise some virtuous lie
To do more for me than mine own desert,
And hang more praise upon deceased I
Than niggard truth would willingly impart.
O, lest your true love may seem false in this,
That you for love speak well of me untrue,
My name be buried where my body is,
And live no more to shame nor me nor you;
    For I am sham'd by that which I bring forth,
    And so should you, to love things nothing worth.

1 *task*] require; *recite*] tell 4 *prove*] discover 6 *desert*] merit 8 *niggard*] miserly; *impart*] give out 10 *untrue*] without truth 11 *My name be*] let my name be 13 *that which I bring forth*] (my verses and plays? your love for me?) 14 *should you*] should you be ashamed

73

That time of year thou mayst in me behold
When yellow leaves, or none, or few, do hang
Upon those boughs which shake against the cold,
Bare ruin'd choirs where late the sweet birds sang.
In me thou seest the twilight of such day
As after sunset fadeth in the west;
Which by and by black night doth take away,
Death's second self, that seals up all in rest.
In me thou seest the glowing of such fire
That on the ashes of his youth doth lie,
As the death-bed whereon it must expire,
Consum'd with that which it was nourish'd by.
    This thou perceiv'st, which makes thy love more strong,
    To love that well which thou must leave ere long.

4 *choirs*] in churches, where divine service is sung 8 *seals up*] (as in a coffin) 10 *his*] its

74

But be contented when that fell arrest
Without all bail shall carry me away.
My life hath in this line some interest,
Which for memorial still with thee shall stay.
When thou reviewest this, thou dost review
The very part was consecrate to thee.
The earth can have but earth, which is his due;
My spirit is thine, the better part of me.
So then thou hast but lost the dregs of life,
The prey of worms, my body being dead,
The coward conquest of a wretch's knife,
Too base of thee to be remembered.
    The worth of that is that which it contains,
    And that is this, and this with thee remains.

1 *fell*] cruel; *arrest*] taking into custody 2 *bail*] possibility of release 3 *line*] (of verse); *interest*] part 4 *memorial*] reminder 6 *part was consecrate*] part that was devoted 7 *his*] its 9 *but*] only 11 *The coward conquest of*] a thing that can in cowardly fashion be conquered by 12 *of*] by 13 The value of the body lies in the spirit it contains 14 *And that is this*] and the spirit is this poetry

75

So are you to my thoughts as food to life,
Or as sweet-season'd showers are to the ground;
And for the peace of you I hold such strife
As 'twixt a miser and his wealth is found,
Now proud as an enjoyer, and anon
Doubting the filching age will steal his treasure;
Now counting best to be with you alone,
Then better'd that the world may see my pleasure;
Sometime all full with feasting on your sight,
And by and by clean starved for a look;
Possessing or pursuing no delight
Save what is had or must from you be took.
Thus do I pine and surfeit day by day,
Or gluttoning on all, or all away.

2 *sweet-season'd showers*] temperate showers, showers of the spring 3 *for the peace of you*] for the sake of the peace you bring me, or the peace that you possess 5 *enjoyer*] possessor 6 *Doubting*] fearing; *filching*] thievish 7 *counting*] thinking it 8 *better'd*] thinking it better 10 *clean*] entirely 14 *Or . . . or*] either . . . or; *all away*] having nothing at all

76

Why is my verse so barren of new pride,
So far from variation or quick change?
Why with the time do I not glance aside
To new-found methods and to compounds strange?
Why write I still all one, ever the same,
And keep invention in a noted weed,
That every word doth almost tell my name,
Showing their birth, and where they did proceed?
O, know, sweet love, I always write of you,
And you and love are still my argument;
So all my best is dressing old words new,
Spending again what is already spent;
    For as the sun is daily new and old,
    So is my love, still telling what is told.

1 *barren of new pride*] lacking in novel ornament 2 *quick*] lively 3 *with the time*] in accordance with fashion 4 *methods*] ways of proceeding; *compounds strange*] exotic compound phrases 5 *still all one*] always the same 6 *invention*] poetic subject-matter; *noted weed*] familiar dress 8 *where*] from where

77

Thy glass will show thee how thy beauties wear,
Thy dial how thy precious minutes waste;
The vacant leaves thy mind's imprint will bear,
And of this book this learning mayst thou taste:
The wrinkles which thy glass will truly show
Of mouthed graves will give thee memory;
Thou by thy dial's shady stealth mayst know
Time's thievish progress to eternity;
Look, what thy memory cannot contain
Commit to these waste blanks, and thou shalt find
Those children nurs'd, deliver'd from thy brain,
To take a new acquaintance of thy mind.
These offices, so oft as thou wilt look,
Shall profit thee and much enrich thy book.

1 *glass*] mirror; *wear*] wear away, last out 2 *dial*] sundial; *waste*] pass away 3 The empty pages will bear the traces of your thought (in writing) 4 *this book*] (This poem seems to have accompanied the gift of a blank notebook); *taste*] sample 6 *mouthed*] i.e. wide-mouthed; *give thee memory*] remind you 7 *thy dial's shady stealth*] the stealthy progress of the shadow on your sundial 10 *waste blanks*] blank pages 11 *children*] i.e. your thoughts 13 *offices*] duties (of consulting mirror, sundial and book)

78

So oft have I invok'd thee for my Muse
And found such fair assistance in my verse
As every alien pen hath got my use,
And under thee their poesy disperse.
Thine eyes, that taught the dumb on high to sing
And heavy ignorance aloft to fly,
Have added feathers to the learned's wing
And given grace a double majesty.
Yet be most proud of that which I compile,
Whose influence is thine and born of thee.
In others' works thou dost but mend the style,
And arts with thy sweet graces graced be;
    But thou art all my art, and dost advance
    As high as learning my rude ignorance.

1 *for*] as 2 *fair*] favourable 3 *As*] that; *alien pen*] pen of a stranger; *got my use*] adopted my practice 4 *under thee*] in your service 8 *grace*] excellence; *double majesty*] double claim to admiration 10 *influence*] inspiration (the allusion is to the influence supposed to derive from stars) 11 *mend*] improve 12 *graced*] beautified 14 *rude*] simple, crude

79

Whilst I alone did call upon thy aid,
My verse alone had all thy gentle grace;
But now my gracious numbers are decay'd,
And my sick Muse doth give another place.
I grant, sweet love, thy lovely argument
Deserves the travail of a worthier pen,
Yet what of thee thy poet doth invent
He robs thee of, and pays it thee again.
He lends thee virtue, and he stole that word
From thy behaviour; beauty doth he give,
And found it in thy cheek: he can afford
No praise to thee but what in thee doth live.
    Then thank him not for that which he doth say,
    Since what he owes thee thou thyself dost pay.

2 *gentle grace*] courteous favour 3 *numbers*] verses 4 *give another place*] give way to someone else 5 *thy lovely argument*] the subject for writing which you in your loveliness constitute 6 *travail*] labour 7 *invent*] devise 9 *lends*] attributes to 10 *behaviour*] bearing, conduct 14 *what he owes thee*] what it is his duty to pay you

80

O, how I faint when I of you do write,
Knowing a better spirit doth use your name,
And in the praise thereof spends all his might
To make me tongue-tied speaking of your fame!
But since your worth, wide as the ocean is,
The humble as the proudest sail doth bear,
My saucy bark, inferior far to his,
On your broad main doth wilfully appear.
Your shallowest help will hold me up afloat,
Whilst he upon your soundless deep doth ride;
Or, being wreck'd, I am a worthless boat,
He of tall building and of goodly pride.
Then if he thrive and I be cast away,
The worst was this: my love was my decay.

1 *faint*] fail in spirit 2 *spirit*] i.e. poet 4 *To make me*] so that I am made 6 *bear*] tolerate, bear up 7 *saucy*] impertinent; *bark*] small boat 8 *main*] ocean; *wilfully*] obstinately 10 *soundless*] unfathomable 11 *being wreck'd*] if either of us is wrecked 12 *tall building*] sturdy construction; *pride*] splendour 14 *my love was my decay*] my love for you, or you whom I love, caused my downfall

81

Or I shall live your epitaph to make,
Or you survive when I in earth am rotten;
From hence your memory death cannot take,
Although in me each part will be forgotten.
Your name from hence immortal life shall have,
Though I, once gone, to all the world must die.
The earth can yield me but a common grave
When you entombed in men's eyes shall lie.
Your monument shall be my gentle verse,
Which eyes not yet created shall o'er-read;
And tongues to be your being shall rehearse
When all the breathers of this world are dead.
You still shall live – such virtue hath my pen –
Where breath most breathes, even in the mouths of men.

1–2 *Or . . . Or*] Either . . . or 3 *hence*] this world, these lines 4 *in me each part*] every quality of mine 5 *from hence*] henceforth, from these lines 6 *to all the world must die*] will be completely dead (there will be no memory of me) 7 *common*] ordinary 8 *entombed in men's eyes*] in a tomb in the sight of all 11 *rehearse*] repeat 13 *virtue*] power

82

I grant thou wert not married to my Muse,
And therefore mayst without attaint o'erlook
The dedicated words which writers use
Of their fair subject, blessing every book.
Thou art as fair in knowledge as in hue,
Finding thy worth a limit past my praise;
And therefore art enforc'd to seek anew
Some fresher stamp of these time-bett'ring days.
And do so, love; yet when they have devis'd
What strained touches rhetoric can lend,
Thou, truly fair, wert truly sympathiz'd
In true plain words by thy true-telling friend;
    And their gross painting might be better us'd
    Where cheeks need blood: in thee it is abus'd.

2 *attaint*] dishonour 3 *dedicated*] devoted; *writers*] i.e. other writers 5 *in knowledge as in hue*] in understanding as in appearance 6 When you decide that my praise cannot reach the limits of your worth 8 *time-bett'ring days*] days in which the arts are improving on the past 11 *truly sympathiz'd*] given a true likeness 13 *gross painting*] crude laying on of praise like a cosmetic

83

I never saw that you did painting need,
And therefore to your fair no painting set;
I found, or thought I found, you did exceed
The barren tender of a poet's debt;
And therefore have I slept in your report,
That you yourself, being extant, well might show
How far a modern quill doth come too short,
Speaking of worth, what worth in you doth grow.
This silence for my sin you did impute,
Which shall be most my glory, being dumb;
For I impair not beauty, being mute,
When others would give life, and bring a tomb.
  There lives more life in one of your fair eyes
  Than both your poets can in praise devise.

1 *painting*] (as in the previous sonnet) 2 *fair*] beauty 4 The worthless tribute of poet to patron 5 *slept in your report*] been inactive in publishing your virtues 6 *That*] because; *extant*] in existence 7 *modern*] ordinary, of the present times 9 *for*] as 11 *being mute*] by being silent 14 *both your poets*] the writer and his rival

84

Who is it that says most, which can say more
Than this rich praise, that you alone are you,
In whose confine immured is the store
Which should example where your equal grew?
Lean penury within that pen doth dwell
That to his subject lends not some small glory;
But he that writes of you, if he can tell
That you are you, so dignifies his story.
Let him but copy what in you is writ,
Not making worse what Nature made so clear,
And such a counterpart shall fame his wit,
Making his style admired everywhere.
You to your beauteous blessings add a curse,
Being fond on praise, which makes your praises worse.

1 Whoever says most can say no more 3–4 Within whom is confined the abundance of quality which should serve as a model for your equal 8 *so*] in that way 10 *clear*] without blemish 11 *counterpart*] likeness; *fame his wit*] make his intellectual and creative powers famous 14 *on*] of; *which makes your praises worse*] (because it encourages attempts to improve upon your perfection in praise, and so to diminish it)

85

My tongue-tied Muse in manners holds her still
While comments of your praise, richly compil'd,
Reserve thy character with golden quill
And precious phrase by all the Muses fil'd.
I think good thoughts whilst other write good words,
And like unletter'd clerk still cry 'Amen'
To every hymn that able spirit affords
In polish'd form of well-refined pen.
Hearing you prais'd I say ''Tis so, 'tis true,'
And to the most of praise add something more;
But that is in my thought, whose love to you,
Though words come hindmost, holds his rank before.
    Then others for the breath of words respect,
    Me for my dumb thoughts, speaking in effect.

1 *in manners holds her still*] politely keeps silence 2 *comments of your praise*] treatises in your praise 3 *Reserve thy character*] preserve your character (so far that it is reflected in the *character* of their handwriting) 4 *fil'd*] polished 6 *unletter'd*] illiterate 7 *able spirit*] accomplished poet 8 *well-refined pen*] cultivated writer 12 *holds his rank before*] comes first 14 *effect*] deeds

86

Was it the proud full sail of his great verse,
Bound for the prize of all-too-precious you
That did my ripe thoughts in my brain inhearse,
Making their tomb the womb wherein they grew?
Was it his spirit, by spirits taught to write
Above a mortal pitch, that struck me dead?
No, neither he nor his compeers by night
Giving him aid my verse astonished.
He nor that affable familiar ghost
Which nightly gulls him with intelligence,
As victors of my silence cannot boast;
I was not sick of any fear from thence.
  But when your countenance fill'd up his line,
  Then lack'd I matter; that enfeebled mine.

1 *proud*] splendid, arrogant 3 *ripe*] ready for birth; *inhearse*] bury 5 *by spirits taught*] (the spirits that inhabit the great poetry of the past? or literally *spirits*, supernatural beings whom the poet claims to inspire him?) 6 *Above a mortal pitch*] at more than human level 7 *compeers*] associates (either the ancient poets he reads at night or the *spirits* who visit him then) 8 *astonished*] struck dumb 9 *affable familiar ghost*] friendly attendant spirit (*familiar* has sinister undertones) 10 *gulls*] tricks; *intelligence*] superior understanding, privileged information 12 *of*] with 13 *countenance*] face (as subject-matter), approval (of the finished *line*); *fill'd up*] made up for the deficiencies of 14 *matter*] anything to write about

87

Farewell, thou art too dear for my possessing,
And like enough thou know'st thy estimate.
The charter of thy worth gives thee releasing;
My bonds in thee are all determinate.
For how do I hold thee but by thy granting?
And for that riches where is my deserving?
The cause of this fair gift in me is wanting,
And so my patent back again is swerving.
Thyself thou gav'st, thy own worth then not knowing,
Or me to whom thou gav'st it else mistaking;
So thy great gift, upon misprision growing,
Comes home again, on better judgement making.
Thus have I had thee as a dream doth flatter:
In sleep a king, but waking no such matter.

1 *art too dear*] cost too much in pains, are too much loved by me (and/or others) 2 *estimate*] value 3 *charter of thy worth*] privilege conferred by your high value or creating that value in the eyes of the world; *releasing*] exemption 4 *bonds*] ties (with suggestions of legal contract and of slavery); *determinate*] ended 7 *wanting*] lacking 8 And so my claim to ownership reverts to you 10 *me . . . mistaking*] taking me for other than I was 11 *upon misprision growing*] based on misunderstanding or error

88

When thou shalt be dispos'd to set me light
And place my merit in the eye of scorn,
Upon thy side against myself I'll fight,
And prove thee virtuous though thou art forsworn.
With mine own weakness being best acquainted,
Upon thy part I can set down a story
Of faults conceal'd, wherein I am attainted,
That thou in losing me shall win much glory,
And I by this will be a gainer too;
For bending all my loving thoughts on thee,
The injuries that to myself I do,
Doing thee vantage, double-vantage me.
Such is my love, to thee I so belong,
That for thy right myself will bear all wrong.

1 *set me light*] value me little 2 And expose my merits to scorn 6 *Upon thy part*] in your support 7 *attainted*] dishonoured 8 *That*] so that 10 *Bending . . . on*] directing . . . towards 12 Because they benefit you, bring me a double benefit

89

Say that thou didst forsake me for some fault,
And I will comment upon that offence;
Speak of my lameness, and I straight will halt,
Against thy reasons making no defence.
Thou canst not, love, disgrace me half so ill,
To set a form upon desired change,
As I'll myself disgrace, knowing thy will.
I will acquaintance strangle and look strange,
Be absent from thy walks, and in my tongue
Thy sweet beloved name no more shall dwell,
Lest I, too much profane, should do it wrong,
And haply of our old acquaintance tell.
    For thee, against myself I'll vow debate;
    For I must ne'er love him whom thou dost hate.

2 *comment*] expound 3 *halt*] limp 5 *disgrace*] discredit 6 To offer acceptable reason for the change you wish 8 *acquaintance strangle*] deny familiarity with you; *strange*] as though I did not know you 9 *thy walks*] where you pass 11 *too much profane*] too little worthy, so far from your divine merit 12 *haply*] by chance 13 *vow debate*] promise to fight

90

Then hate me when thou wilt; if ever, now;
Now, while the world is bent my deeds to cross,
Join with the spite of fortune, make me bow,
And do not drop in for an after-loss.
Ah, do not, when my heart hath scap'd this sorrow,
Come in the rearward of a conquer'd woe;
Give not a windy night a rainy morrow,
To linger out a purpos'd overthrow.
If thou wilt leave me, do not leave me last,
When other petty griefs have done their spite,
But in the onset come; so shall I taste
At first the very worst of fortune's might,
    And other strains of woe, which now seem woe,
    Compar'd with loss of thee will not seem so.

1 *Then*] therefore (following on from Sonnet 89) 4 *drop in for an after-loss*] fall on me as a loss following all the others 5 *scap'd this sorrow*] survived my present trouble 6 *rearward*] rearguard 8 *linger out*] prolong; *purpos'd overthrow*] reversal of fortune intended me 11 *in the onset*] at the start, in the front of the attackers 13 *strains*] kinds

91

Some glory in their birth, some in their skill,
Some in their wealth, some in their body's force,
Some in their garments (though new-fangled ill),
Some in their hawks and hounds, some in their horse;
And every humour hath his adjunct pleasure,
Wherein it finds a joy above the rest.
But these particulars are not my measure;
All these I better in one general best.
Thy love is better than high birth to me,
Richer than wealth, prouder than garments' cost,
Of more delight than hawks or horses be;
And having thee of all men's pride I boast –
    Wretched in this alone, that thou mayst take
    All this away, and me most wretched make.

2 *force*] strength   5 *adjunct*] associated   12 *all men's pride*] all the things which men take pride in

92

But do thy worst to steal thyself away,
For term of life thou art assured mine,
And life no longer than thy love will stay;
For it depends upon that love of thine.
Then need I not to fear the worst of wrongs
When in the least of them my life hath end.
I see a better state to me belongs
Than that which on thy humour doth depend.
Thou canst not vex me with inconstant mind,
Since that my life on thy revolt doth lie.
O, what a happy title do I find,
Happy to have thy love, happy to die!
But what's so blessed fair that fears no blot?
Thou mayst be false, and yet I know it not.

This follows on from the previous sonnet. 2 *assured*] pledged 6 *least of them*] least wrong you can do me 8 *humour*] mood, caprice 10 *on thy revolt doth lie*] is at stake if you turn away from me 11 *title*] claim to possession

93

So shall I live supposing thou art true,
Like a deceived husband; so love's face
May still seem love to me, though alter'd new,
Thy looks with me, thy heart in other place.
For there can live no hatred in thine eye,
Therefore in that I cannot know thy change.
In many's looks the false heart's history
Is writ in moods and frowns and wrinkles strange,
But heaven in thy creation did decree
That in thy face sweet love should ever dwell;
Whate'er thy thoughts or thy heart's workings be,
Thy looks should nothing thence but sweetness tell.
    How like Eve's apple doth thy beauty grow,
    If thy sweet virtue answer not thy show!

This follows on from the previous sonnet. 1 *supposing*] imagining
2 *face*] appearance 7 *many's looks*] the looks of many people

94

They that have power to hurt, and will do none,
That do not do the thing they most do show,
Who, moving others, are themselves as stone,
Unmoved, cold, and to temptation slow –
They rightly do inherit heaven's graces,
And husband nature's riches from expense;
They are the lords and owners of their faces,
Others but stewards of their excellence.
The summer's flower is to the summer sweet,
Though to itself it only live and die,
But if that flower with base infection meet,
The basest weed outbraves his dignity;
    For sweetest things turn sourest by their deeds:
    Lilies that fester smell far worse than weeds.

2 *the thing they most do show*] what they seem most likely to do from their appearance (some suggestion of hypocrisy, developing as the poem continues) 5 *rightly*] (ironic tone possible); *graces*] favours (in looks and otherwise) 6 *husband*] manage prudently; *expense*] being wastefully expended 8 *stewards*] caretakers, custodians 9 *is to the summer sweet*] perfumes the summer air 10 *to itself*] in isolation, without reference to others 11 *base*] loathsome 12 *basest*] lowliest; *outbraves*] surpasses (in appearance or moral quality)

95

How sweet and lovely dost thou make the shame
Which, like a canker in the fragrant rose,
Doth spot the beauty of thy budding name!
O, in what sweets dost thou thy sins enclose!
That tongue that tells the story of thy days,
Making lascivious comments on thy sport,
Cannot dispraise, but in a kind of praise,
Naming thy name, blesses an ill report.
O, what a mansion have those vices got
Which for their habitation chose out thee,
Where beauty's veil doth cover every blot,
And all things turns to fair that eyes can see!
    Take heed, dear heart, of this large privilege:
    The hardest knife ill-us'd doth lose his edge.

2 *canker*] grub causing blight 3 *name*] reputation 6 *sport*] (sexual) fun 7–8 The ambiguous punctuation (the two lines may or may not be independent of each other) follows the earliest text 12 (The subject of *turns* is *beauty's veil*) 14 *his*] its

96

Some say thy fault is youth, some wantonness,
Some say thy grace is youth and gentle sport.
Both grace and faults are lov'd of more and less;
Thou mak'st faults graces that to thee resort.
As on the finger of a throned queen
The basest jewel will be well esteem'd,
So are those errors that in thee are seen
To truths translated, and for true things deem'd.
How many lambs might the stern wolf betray
If like a lamb he could his looks translate!
How many gazers mightst thou lead away
If thou wouldst use the strength of all thy state!
    But do not so. I love thee in such sort
    As, thou being mine, mine is thy good report.

1 *wantonness*] playful extravagance, immoral sexuality 2 *gentle*] becoming a gentleman 3 *of more and less*] by all classes of people 8 *translated*] transformed; *deem'd*] judged 9 *betray*] deceive to their misfortune 12 *state*] pre-eminent position 13–14 These lines also conclude Sonnet 36 14 *report*] reputation

97

How like a winter hath my absence been
From thee, the pleasure of the fleeting year!
What freezings have I felt, what dark days seen,
What old December's bareness everywhere!
And yet this time remov'd was summer's time,
The teeming autumn big with rich increase,
Bearing the wanton burden of the prime
Like widow'd wombs after their lords' decease.
Yet this abundant issue seem'd to me
But hope of orphans and unfather'd fruit,
For summer and his pleasures wait on thee,
And thou away, the very birds are mute;
    Or if they sing, 'tis with so dull a cheer
    That leaves look pale, dreading the winter's near.

2 *the pleasure of*] what pleases most in, what is most pleasing to; *fleeting*] swiftly passing 5 *time remov'd*] time of separation; *summer's time*] time for summer to bring forth autumn (as though autumn were summer's child) 6 *teeming*] prolific; *increase*] (stressed on the second syllable) 7 *wanton burden*] i.e. offspring, conceived in pleasure and bringing pleasure; *prime*] spring 11 *his*] its; *wait on*] follow

98

From you have I been absent in the spring
When proud pied April, dress'd in all his trim,
Hath put a spirit of youth in everything,
That heavy Saturn laugh'd and leapt with him.
Yet nor the lays of birds nor the sweet smell
Of different flowers in odour and in hue
Could make me any summer's story tell,
Or from their proud lap pluck them where they grew;
Nor did I wonder at the lily's white,
Nor praise the deep vermilion in the rose.
They were but sweet, but figures of delight
Drawn after you, you pattern of all those;
    Yet seem'd it winter still, and, you away,
    As with your shadow I with these did play.

2 *proud pied*] fine and many-coloured; *trim*] bravery 4 *That*] with the result that; *heavy Saturn*] the ponderous god (and planet) of melancholy 5 *Yet nor the lays*] yet neither the songs 7 *any summer's story tell*] speak cheerfully or of cheerful things 8 *proud*] brilliant; *lap*] i.e. the earth 11 *figures*] secondary representatives 12 *after you*] in your likeness

102

My love is strengthen'd, though more weak in seeming.
I love not less, though less the show appear.
That love is merchandiz'd whose rich esteeming
The owner's tongue doth publish everywhere.
Our love was new and then but in the spring
When I was wont to greet it with my lays,
As Philomel in summer's front doth sing,
And stops her pipe in growth of riper days –
Not that the summer is less pleasant now
Than when her mournful hymns did hush the night,
But that wild music burdens every bough,
And sweets grown common lose their dear delight.
  Therefore like her I sometime hold my tongue,
  Because I would not dull you with my song.

3 *rich esteeming*] high valuation 4 *publish*] make public 6 *lays*] songs 7 *Philomel*] the nightingale; *in summer's front*] at the start of summer 8 *her pipe*] her singing; *in growth . . . days*] as summer comes into its own 10 *her*] the nightingale's 14 *dull*] bore, make dull

104

To me, fair friend, you never can be old;
For as you were when first your eye I eyed,
Such seems your beauty still. Three winters cold
Have from the forests shook three summers' pride;
Three beauteous springs to yellow autumn turn'd
In process of the seasons have I seen,
Three April perfumes in three hot Junes burn'd
Since first I saw you fresh, which yet are green.
Ah yet doth beauty like a dial-hand
Steal from his figure, and no pace perceiv'd;
So your sweet hue, which methinks still doth stand,
Hath motion, and mine eye may be deceiv'd.
For fear of which, hear this, thou age unbred:
Ere you were born was beauty's summer dead.

4 *pride*] fine show 8 *yet*] still; *green*] vigorously youthful 9 *dial-hand*] hand of a clock 10 *Steal*] steal away; *figure*] number on the clock face, bodily form 11 *hue*] complexion; *methinks still doth stand*] seems to me the same as it was, not to change 13 *unbred*] unborn, yet to come

106

When in the chronicle of wasted time
I see descriptions of the fairest wights,
And beauty making beautiful old rhyme
In praise of ladies dead and lovely knights;
Then in the blazon of sweet beauty's best,
Of hand, of foot, of lip, of eye, of brow,
I see their antique pen would have express'd
Even such a beauty as you master now.
So all their praises are but prophecies
Of this our time, all you prefiguring,
And for they look'd but with divining eyes,
They had not skill enough your worth to sing;
    For we which now behold these present days
    Have eyes to wonder, but lack tongues to praise.

1 *wasted*] past, laid waste 2 *wights*] people (archaic in Shakespeare's time) 5 *blazon*] record, memorial (with heraldic associations) 7 *antique*] (stress on the first syllable) 11 *divining*] forecasting without certainty

107

Not mine own fears, nor the prophetic soul
Of the wide world dreaming on things to come,
Can yet the lease of my true love control,
Suppos'd as forfeit to a confin'd doom.
The mortal moon hath her eclipse endur'd,
And the sad augurs mock their own presage;
Incertainties now crown themselves assur'd,
And peace proclaims olives of endless age.
Now with the drops of this most balmy time
My love looks fresh, and Death to me subscribes,
Since spite of him I'll live in this poor rhyme
While he insults o'er dull and speechless tribes.
    And thou in this shalt find thy monument
    When tyrants' crests and tombs of brass are spent.

This sonnet evidently alludes to events in 'the wide world' – but which? It would not be appropriate here to rehearse the many theories. I take the view that the 'mortal moon' is not the line of battle of the Armada in 1588, nor literally the moon, which underwent an eclipse in 1595, nor anything or anyone else than Queen Elizabeth I, often compared to Diana, goddess of the moon, who experienced her own mortality when she died in 1603 and was replaced by the peace-maker, James I. 1 *prophetic soul*] collective consciousness anxiously anticipating the future 3 *lease*] time allotted; *control*] check, put a limit to 4 Thought subject to termination within an allotted period 6 *sad*] grave, grief-stricken; *mock . . . presage*] are scornful of their own predictions 7 What was uncertain (the succession to Elizabeth?) is no longer so (James will be crowned?) 8 *olives . . . age*] olive branches (symbols of peace) that will last for ever 9 *drops*] tears of joy and grief, medicines; *balmy*] fragrant and healthful 10 *fresh*] young and vigorous; *to me subscribes*] acknowledges me his superior 12 *insults*] triumphs; *speechless*] (because making no rhymes) 14 *spent*] ruined

108

What's in the brain that ink may character
Which hath not figur'd to thee my true spirit?
What's new to speak, what now to register,
That may express my love or thy dear merit?
Nothing, sweet boy; but yet, like prayers divine,
I must each day say o'er the very same,
Counting no old thing old, thou mine, I thine,
Even as when first I hallow'd thy fair name.
So that eternal love in love's fresh case
Weighs not the dust and injury of age,
Nor gives to necessary wrinkles place,
But makes antiquity for aye his page,
    Finding the first conceit of love there bred
    Where time and outward form would show it dead.

1 *character*] put into writing 2 *figur'd*] represented 8 *hallow'd*] blessed 9 *fresh case*] lively state, spruce dress 10 *Weighs not*] takes no account of 12 But makes of age his ever-young servant 13 *first conceit of love*] love in its original force 14 *would show it*] make it appear, wish it to appear

109

O never say that I was false of heart,
Though absence seem'd my flame to qualify.
As easy might I from myself depart
As from my soul, which in thy breast doth lie;
That is my home of love. If I have rang'd,
Like him that travels, I return again,
Just to the time, not with the time exchang'd,
So that myself bring water for my stain.
Never believe, though in my nature reign'd
All frailties that besiege all kinds of blood,
That it could so preposterously be stain'd
To leave for nothing all thy sum of good;
    For nothing this wide universe I call,
    Save thou, my rose; in it thou art my all.

2 *my flame to qualify*] to diminish my love for you 5 *rang'd*] wandered
7 True to my appointed hour and not changed by the passage of time
10 *kinds of blood*] i.e. temperaments 11 *preposterously*] unnaturally

110

Alas, 'tis true, I have gone here and there
And made myself a motley to the view,
Gor'd mine own thoughts, sold cheap what is most dear,
Made old offences of affections new.
Most true it is that I have look'd on truth
Askance and strangely; but, by all above,
These blenches gave my heart another youth,
And worse essays prov'd thee my best of love.
Now all is done, have what shall have no end:
Mine appetite I never more will grind
On newer proof, to try an older friend,
A god in love, to whom I am confin'd.
Then give me welcome, next my heaven the best,
Even to thy pure and most most loving breast.

2 *a motley to the view*] visibly a fool ('motley' is the characteristic dress of fools) 3 *Gor'd*] wounded, tricked out in 'gores' (the triangular pieces of cloth that are part of 'motley') 4 Given new instances of my old offence of unfaithfulness 6 *strangely*] as though without recognition 7 *blenches*] ?foolish tricks (a very difficult word to gloss, apparently combining ideas of trickery and game with that of a feint or swerve from the direct line) 8 *worse essays*] experience of an inferior love 10 *grind*] whet, sharpen 11 *On newer proof*] by experiment with the new 12 *confin'd*] bound 13 *next my heaven the best*] the best welcome, next to you, my heaven

111

O, for my sake do you with Fortune chide,
The guilty goddess of my harmful deeds,
That did not better for my life provide
Than public means which public manners breeds.
Thence comes it that my name receives a brand,
And almost thence my nature is subdu'd
To what it works in, like the dyer's hand.
Pity me then, and wish I were renew'd,
Whilst, like a willing patient, I will drink
Potions of eisel 'gainst my strong infection;
No bitterness that I will bitter think,
Nor double penance to correct correction.
Pity me then, dear friend, and I assure ye
Even that your pity is enough to cure me.

2 *guilty*] (Fortune shares in the guilt of the deeds she encouraged) 3 *life*] livelihood 4 *public means*] a living made in the public world; *public manners breeds*] generates vulgar, showy behaviour 5 *brand*] stigma 6–7 *subdu'd/ To*] overpowered by 10 *eisel*] vinegar (taken against the plague) 11 *No bitterness*] there is no bitterness 12 *to correct correction*] to correct further what has been corrected already by a first penance

112

Your love and pity doth th'impression fill
Which vulgar scandal stamp'd upon my brow;
For what care I who calls me well or ill,
So you o'er-green my bad, my good allow?
You are my all the world, and I must strive
To know my shames and praises from your tongue;
None else to me, nor I to none alive,
That my steel'd sense or changes right or wrong.
In so profound abysm I throw all care
Of others' voices that my adder's sense
To critic and to flatterer stopped are.
Mark how with my neglect I do dispense:
  You are so strongly in my purpose bred
  That all the world besides, methinks th'are dead.

1 *impression*] i.e. scar (cf. the *brand* of the previous sonnet) 2 *vulgar scandal*] public disgrace, common slander; *stamp'd*] i.e. branded 4 *o'er-green*] cover with fresh and healthy growth; *allow*] approve 7–8 There is no one else alive who matters for me, or to whom I matter, who affects my obdurate sense, for right or wrong 9 *In so profound*] into so deep an 10 *adder's sense*] (The adder was proverbially deaf) 12 *with . . . dispense*] I excuse my neglect (of others' voices) 13 *in my purpose bred*] cherished in and by my committed self 14 *th'are*] they (i.e. all the world besides) are

114

Or whether doth my mind, being crown'd with you,
Drink up the monarch's plague, this flattery?
Or whether shall I say mine eye saith true,
And that your love taught it this alchemy,
To make of monsters and things indigest
Such cherubins as your sweet self resemble,
Creating every bad a perfect best
As fast as objects to his beams assemble?
O, 'tis the first, 'tis flattery in my seeing,
And my great mind most kingly drinks it up.
Mine eye well knows what with his gust is 'greeing,
And to his palate doth prepare the cup.
    If it be poison'd, 'tis the lesser sin
    That mine eye loves it and doth first begin.

1, 3 *Or whether . . . Or whether*] (indicates alternative questions) 1 *crown'd with you*] made a king by your love 5 *indigest*] shapeless 8 As fast as objects come within my gaze 9 *flattery*] (2 syllables here, though 3 in line 2) 10 *most kingly*] in perfect royal fashion 11 *what with . . . 'greeing*] what is to my mind's taste 12 *to*] to please 14 *doth first begin*] drinks first

115

Those lines that I before have writ do lie,
Even those that said I could not love you dearer;
Yet then my judgement knew no reason why
My most full flame should afterwards burn clearer.
But reckoning Time, whose million'd accidents
Creep in 'twixt vows and change decrees of kings,
Tan sacred beauty, blunt the sharp'st intents,
Divert strong minds to th'course of alt'ring things –
Alas, why, fearing of Time's tyranny,
Might I not then say 'Now I love you best',
When I was certain o'er incertainty,
Crowning the present, doubting of the rest?
  Love is a babe; then might I not say so,
  To give full growth to that which still doth grow.

5 *accidents*] occurrences 7 *Tan*] darken, turn leathery 8 *course*] way (here, perhaps with the suggestion of a water-course) 11 *o'er incertainty*] despite others' doubts, despite my own doubts about the future, despite the uncertain nature of the world 12 *Crowning the present*] making the present a royal time, treating it as though it were 13 *babe*] (because Cupid is so depicted); *then*] therefore, at that time 14 Because it suggested that my love, which is still growing, had reached its fullest maturity

116

Let me not to the marriage of true minds
Admit impediments. Love is not love
Which alters when it alteration finds,
Or bends with the remover to remove.
O no, it is an ever-fixed mark
That looks on tempests and is never shaken;
It is the star to every wand'ring bark,
Whose worth's unknown although his height be taken.
Love's not Time's fool, though rosy lips and cheeks
Within his bending sickle's compass come;
Love alters not with his brief hours and weeks,
But bears it out even to the edge of doom.
If this be error and upon me prov'd,
I never writ, nor no man ever lov'd.

2 *Admit*] allow consideration of 3–4 That changes when it discovers change (in the appearance or affections of the loved one), or alters course if the loved one turns elsewhere 5 *mark*] sea-mark (here, a star by which bearings are to be taken) 7 *bark*] boat 8 *worth*] value, quality (and hence, perhaps, true nature); *his . . . taken*] its altitude be measured (the height of the pole star being an indication of latitude, and so an indication of where a boat is) 9 *Time's fool*] made a mock of by Time 12 *bears it out*] endures; *edge of doom*] judgement-day

117

Accuse me thus: that I have scanted all
Wherein I should your great deserts repay,
Forgot upon your dearest love to call,
Whereto all bonds do tie me day by day;
That I have frequent been with unknown minds,
And given to time your own dear-purchas'd right;
That I have hoisted sail to all the winds
Which should transport me farthest from your sight.
Book both my wilfulness and errors down,
And on just proof surmise accumulate;
Bring me within the level of your frown,
But shoot not at me in your waken'd hate,
  Since my appeal says I did strive to prove
  The constancy and virtue of your love.

1 *scanted*] given short measure in 2 *great deserts*] many and excellent qualities deserving of my love 5 *frequent*] familiar; *unknown minds*] strangers, people unknown to you, of no significance 6 *given . . . right*] wasted the time which was yours by virtue of your dearest love 9 *Book . . . down*] put on record 10 *on just . . . accumulate*] add what you suspect to what you have certain proof of 11 *level*] aim (as of a weapon) 13 *appeal*] plea (in mitigation); *prove*] test

118

Like as, to make our appetites more keen,
With eager compounds we our palate urge;
As, to prevent our maladies unseen,
We sicken to shun sickness when we purge;
Even so, being full of your ne'er-cloying sweetness,
To bitter sauces did I frame my feeding;
And, sick of welfare, found a kind of meetness
To be diseas'd ere that there was true needing.
Thus policy in love, t' anticipate
The ills that were not, grew to faults assur'd,
And brought to medicine a healthful state
Which, rank of goodness, would by ill be cur'd.
    But thence I learn, and find the lesson true:
    Drugs poison him that so fell sick of you.

1 *Like as*] just as 2 *eager compounds*] sharp sauces or medicinal mixtures; *urge*] stimulate 3 *prevent*] forestall; *unseen*] not yet detected 4 *sicken*] make ourselves ill; *purge*] take laxative medicine 6 *frame my feeding*] direct my diet 7 *welfare*] health 9 *policy*] cunning, (mistaken) prudence 10 *grew to faults assur'd*] developed indubitable illness 11 *medicine*] i.e. need of medicine 12 *rank of*] surfeited with

119

What potions have I drunk of siren tears
Distill'd from limbecks foul as hell within,
Applying fears to hopes and hopes to fears,
Still losing when I saw myself to win!
What wretched errors hath my heart committed
Whilst it hath thought itself so blessed never!
How have mine eyes out of their spheres been fitted
In the distraction of this madding fever!
O benefit of ill! Now I find true
That better is by evil still made better,
And ruin'd love when it is built anew
Grows fairer than at first, more strong, far greater.
  So I return rebuk'd to my content,
  And gain by ills thrice more than I have spent.

1 *potions*] medicinal draughts; *siren*] alluring 2 *limbecks*] alembics, stills 3 *Applying*] (as 'potions' are applied to sicknesses) 6 *so blessed never*] happy as never before 7 *spheres*] sockets; *fitted*] driven by fits 8 *of this madding fever*] caused by the fever of this madness 9 *ill*] sickness, doing wrong 13 *to my content*] (return) to what makes me happy, (rebuked) in a way that pleases me (from its outcome)

120

That you were once unkind befriends me now,
And for that sorrow which I then did feel
Needs must I under my transgression bow,
Unless my nerves were brass or hammer'd steel.
For if you were by my unkindness shaken
As I by yours, y'have pass'd a hell of time,
And I, a tyrant, have no leisure taken
To weigh how once I suffer'd in your crime.
O that our night of woe might have remember'd
My deepest sense how hard true sorrow hits,
And soon to you, as you to me then, tender'd
The humble salve which wounded bosoms fits!
    But that your trespass now becomes a fee;
    Mine ransoms yours, and yours must ransom me.

2 *for*] on account of 3 *under my transgression bow*] submit to a sense of my own wrong-doing 4 *nerves*] sinews, feelings 7–8 *have no . . . weigh*] have not taken the time to reflect 8 *in your crime*] at your wrong behaviour to me 9 *night of woe*] dark time of sorrow; *remember'd*] brought back to mind 11 And that I had speedily offered to you, as you did to me then 12 *humble salve*] remedy of humility, simple remedy; *bosoms*] i.e. hearts 13 *your trespass*] the wrong you did; *fee*] payment, reward 14 *ransoms . . . ransom*] pays for . . . redeem

121

'Tis better to be vile than vile esteem'd,
When not to be receives reproach of being,
And the just pleasure lost, which is so deem'd
Not by our feeling but by others' seeing.
For why should others' false adulterate eyes
Give salutation to my sportive blood?
Or on my frailties why are frailer spies,
Which in their wills count bad what I think good?
No, I am that I am, and they that level
At my abuses reckon up their own;
I may be straight, though they themselves be bevel –
By their rank thoughts my deeds must not be shown,
    Unless this general evil they maintain:
    All men are bad and in their badness reign.

2 *not to be*] i.e. not being vile 3 *just*] legitimate, honourable; *so deem'd*] judged to be vile 5 *adulterate*] impure 6 Greet with familiarity (the actions of) my impetuously expressive love (the line is especially difficult to gloss – there is a suggestion of unpleasantly knowing looks from the 'adulterate eyes', and 'sportive' hovers between ideas of innocent play and guilty sexuality) 7 *why are*] why are there set 8 *wills*] conduct of the will, wilfulness 9 *level*] guess, aim (as with a weapon) 10 *abuses*] misdeeds 11 *bevel*] not straight, at a slant 12 *By*] by analogy with; *rank*] lustful, coarse 14 *in their badness reign*] are royal in nature despite their badness, succeed by being bad

123

No, Time, thou shalt not boast that I do change;
Thy pyramids built up with newer might
To me are nothing novel, nothing strange;
They are but dressings of a former sight.
Our dates are brief, and therefore we admire
What thou dost foist upon us that is old,
And rather make them born to our desire
Than think that we before have heard them told.
Thy registers and thee I both defy,
Not wond'ring at the present nor the past;
For thy records and what we see doth lie,
Made more or less by thy continual haste.
    This I do vow, and this shall ever be:
    I will be true despite thy scythe and thee.

2 *pyramids*] great structures; *newer might*] new force 4 *dressings of*] elaborations on 5 *Our dates*] period of time allowed us 7 *make . . . desire*] imagine them new because we want them to be so 9 *registers*] chronicles 11 *doth lie*] i.e. do lie 12 *more or less*] i.e. more or less significant; *by*] as a result of

124

If my dear love were but the child of state,
It might for Fortune's bastard be unfather'd,
As subject to Time's love or to Time's hate,
Weeds among weeds or flowers with flowers gather'd.
No, it was builded far from accident,
It suffers not in smiling pomp, nor falls
Under the blow of thralled discontent
Whereto th'inviting time our fashion calls.
It fears not Policy, that heretic,
Which works on leases of short-number'd hours,
But all alone stands hugely politic,
That it nor grows with heat nor drowns with showers.
To this I witness call the fools of Time,
Which die for goodness, who have liv'd for crime.

1 *my dear love*] my precious love for the friend; *child of state*] product of circumstance, of his (glamorous) high position 2 *unfather'd*] denied its true paternity, disowned (and made out to be illegitimate offspring) 3 *As*] because 5 *accident*] (the domain of) chance 7 *thralled discontent*] the misery arising from service, from servitude 8 Which the fashion of the time makes attractive to us 9 *Policy*] expediency 10 *on . . . hours*] for and with short-term interests 11 *hugely politic*] massively sagacious 12 *That*] in that; *nor . . . nor*] neither . . . nor 13 *fools of Time*] those who make themselves fools by following the whims of the time, time-servers 14 Who, having lived badly, only manage to do good by dying

125

Were't aught to me I bore the canopy,
With my extern the outward honouring,
Or laid great bases for eternity
Which proves more short than waste or ruining?
Have I not seen dwellers on form and favour
Lose all and more by paying too much rent,
For compound sweet forgoing simple savour,
Pitiful thrivers in their gazing spent?
No, let me be obsequious in thy heart,
And take thou my oblation, poor but free,
Which is not mix'd with seconds, knows no art
But mutual render, only me for thee.
Hence, thou suborn'd informer! A true soul
When most impeach'd stands least in thy control.

1 *Were't aught*] Would it be anything; *bore the canopy*] (in the procession of some great person) 2 *extern*] outward bearing; *outward*] public aspect (of the great person, of affairs) 3 *laid . . . eternity*] made great preparations for enduring achievement 4 Which turns out not to endure as long as decay and destruction 5 *dwellers on*] sticklers for 8 Wretched men though they prosper, used up in feeding their eyes 9 *be obsequious*] offer my service 10 *oblation*] offering; *free*] freely given 11 *mix'd with seconds*] adulterated (the offering is unqualified); *art*] artifice, trickery 12 *But mutual render*] But is the offering up of one to the other and *vice versa* 13 *thou suborn'd informer*] (you who pretend that I am attracted by outward things and who are yourself corrupted, a hired spy) 14 *impeach'd*] accused; *control*] power

126

O thou my lovely boy, who in thy power
Dost hold Time's fickle glass, his sickle hour,
Who hast by waning grown, and therein show'st
Thy lovers withering as thy sweet self grow'st –
If Nature, sovereign mistress over wrack,
As thou goest onwards still will pluck thee back,
She keeps thee to this purpose, that her skill
May Time disgrace, and wretched minutes kill.
Yet fear her, O thou minion of her pleasure!
She may detain but not still keep her treasure.
Her audit, though delay'd, answer'd must be,
And her quietus is to render thee.

Not a defective sonnet, though it is printed like one in the Quarto of 1609, which marks off the 'missing' lines 13 and 14 with brackets; rather, an envoy in six couplets concluding the sequence of sonnets about the friend. 1 *lovely*] beautiful, arousing love 2 *glass*] hour-glass; *sickle hour*] hour that cuts down human life 3 *waning*] growing older (by losing years from his allotted span) 4 *lovers*] (possibly 'lover's') 5 *wrack*] decay 6 *onwards*] (to death); *still*] always, continually 7 *to*] with 8 *disgrace*] dishonour; *kill*] put an end to (the triumph of) 9 *minion*] darling 10 *still*] for ever 11 *audit*] final reckoning; *answer'd*] made 14 *quietus*] discharge

127

In the old age black was not counted fair,
Or if it were, it bore not beauty's name;
But now is black beauty's successive heir,
And beauty slander'd with a bastard shame:
For since each hand hath put on nature's power,
Fairing the foul with art's false borrow'd face,
Sweet beauty hath no name, no holy bower,
But is profan'd, if not lives in disgrace.
Therefore my mistress' eyes are raven-black,
Her brow so suited, and they mourners seem
At such who, not born fair, no beauty lack,
Sland'ring creation with a false esteem.
    Yet so they mourn, becoming of their woe,
    That every tongue says beauty should look so.

1 *age*] days; *fair*] beautiful, not dark 3 *successive*] i.e. legitimate 4 *slander'd . . . shame*] spoken ill of as illegitimate 5 *put on nature's power*] usurped nature's authority 6 *Fairing the foul*] making the ugly beautiful; *art's false borrow'd face*] cosmetics 7 *holy bower*] place where it is reverenced 10 *so suited*] similarly dressed (in black) 11 *no beauty lack*] (because they cheat by using cosmetics) 12 Giving nature a bad name by the false judgments to which they give rise 13 *becoming of*] giving grace to

129

Th'expense of spirit in a waste of shame
Is lust in action; and till action, lust
Is perjur'd, murd'rous, bloody, full of blame,
Savage, extreme, rude, cruel, not to trust,
Enjoy'd no sooner but despised straight,
Past reason hunted, and no sooner had
Past reason hated as a swallowed bait
On purpose laid to make the taker mad;
Mad in pursuit and in possession so,
Had, having, and in quest to have, extreme;
A bliss in proof and prov'd, a very woe;
Before, a joy propos'd; behind, a dream.
All this the world well knows, yet none knows well
To shun the heaven that leads men to this hell.

1 *expense*] using up, paying out; *in a waste of shame*] in the course of shameful extravagance, in a wasteland created by shame 3 *perjur'd*] lying; *full of blame*] greatly to be blamed, very ready to blame (others) 4 *not to trust*] not to be trusted 7 *bait*] (like a rat-poison) 9 *Mad*] (Possibly should be 'Made', as in the 1609 Quarto – i.e. 'made . . . extreme') 11 *in proof*] in the experiencing; *prov'd*] once experienced

130

My mistress' eyes are nothing like the sun;
Coral is far more red than her lips' red.
If snow be white, why then her breasts are dun;
If hairs be wires, black wires grow on her head.
I have seen roses damask'd, red and white,
But no such roses see I in her cheeks;
And in some perfumes is there more delight
Than in the breath that from my mistress reeks.
I love to hear her speak, yet well I know
That music hath a far more pleasing sound.
I grant I never saw a goddess go:
My mistress when she walks treads on the ground.
    And yet, by heaven, I think my love as rare
    As any she belied with false compare.

3 *dun*] dull greyish-brown 5 *damask'd*] i.e. mingling red and white 8 *reeks*] breathes (apparently without the modern sense of a foul smell) 11 *go*] walk 14 *belied*] made the subject of untruth; *false compare*] misleading, deceiving comparison

133

Beshrew that heart that makes my heart to groan
For that deep wound it gives my friend and me!
Is 't not enough to torture me alone,
But slave to slavery my sweet'st friend must be?
Me from myself thy cruel eye hath taken,
And my next self thou harder hast engross'd.
Of him, myself, and thee I am forsaken;
A torment thrice threefold thus to be cross'd.
Prison my heart in thy steel bosom's ward,
But then my friend's heart let my poor heart bail;
Whoe'er keeps me, let my heart be his guard;
Thou canst not then use rigour in my jail.
　　And yet thou wilt; for I, being pent in thee,
　　Perforce am thine, and all that is in me.

1 *Beshrew*] (a mild curse) 2 *For*] on account of 3 *alone*] only 4 *slave to slavery*] enslaved to love (which is itself slavery) 6 *my next self*] my second self, my friend; *harder*] more cruelly; *engross'd*] taken exclusive possession of 8 *cross'd*] frustrated 9 *Prison*] imprison; *ward*] cell 10 *bail*] take responsibility for 12 *use rigour*] exercise cruelty; *my jail*] i.e. my heart, where I guard my friend 13 *pent*] imprisoned

134

So, now I have confess'd that he is thine,
And I myself am mortgag'd to thy will,
Myself I'll forfeit, so that other mine
Thou wilt restore to be my comfort still.
But thou wilt not, nor he will not be free,
For thou art covetous, and he is kind.
He learn'd but surety-like to write for me
Under that bond that him as fast doth bind.
The statute of thy beauty thou wilt take,
Thou usurer that put'st forth all to use,
And sue a friend came debtor for my sake;
So him I lose through my unkind abuse.
 Him have I lost; thou hast both him and me;
 He pays the whole, and yet am I not free.

2 *mortgag'd*] pledged; *to thy will*] to (serve) your will, your sexual appetite 3 *that other mine*] i.e. my friend 4 *restore*] return; *still*] always 5 *nor*] and 6 *covetous*] greedy; *kind*] generous 7 *surety-like . . . me*] to sign his name as a guarantor on my behalf 9 *statute*] all the dues to which your beauty entitles you 10 *that . . . use*] i.e. that have nothing on which you do not seek a return 11 *came*] who became 12 *abuse*] of my friend by my loving you, of me by you

138

When my love swears that she is made of truth,
I do believe her, though I know she lies,
That she might think me some untutor'd youth
Unlearned in the world's false subtleties.
Thus vainly thinking that she thinks me young,
Although she knows my days are past the best,
Simply I credit her false-speaking tongue;
On both sides thus is simple truth suppress'd.
But wherefore says she not she is unjust?
And wherefore say not I that I am old?
O, love's best habit is in seeming trust,
And age in love loves not to have years told.
    Therefore I lie with her, and she with me,
    And in our faults by lies we flatter'd be.

1 *truth*] faithfulness 7 *Simply*] straightforwardly, like a simpleton; *credit*] believe 11 *habit*] way of behaving, dress 12 *told*] counted 13 *lie with*] lie to, make love with 14 *faults*] shortcomings, weakness

140

Be wise as thou art cruel; do not press
My tongue-tied patience with too much disdain,
Lest sorrow lend me words, and words express
The manner of my pity-wanting pain.
If I might teach thee wit, better it were,
Though not to love, yet, love, to tell me so,
As testy sick men, when their deaths be near,
No news but health from their physicians know.
For if I should despair, I should grow mad,
And in my madness might speak ill of thee;
Now this ill-wresting world is grown so bad
Mad sland'rers by mad ears believed be.
　　That I may not be so, nor thou belied,
　　Bear thine eyes straight, though thy proud heart go wide.

1 *press*] oppress, torment 4 *manner*] nature 5 *wit*] good sense 6 *so*] i.e. that you love me 7 *testy*] irritable 11 *ill-wresting*] which puts a bad sense on everything 13 *so*] i.e. believed; *belied*] slandered 14 *wide*] astray

142

Love is my sin, and thy dear virtue hate,
Hate of my sin grounded on sinful loving.
O, but with mine compare thou thine own state,
And thou shalt find it merits not reproving;
Or if it do, not from those lips of thine,
That have profan'd their scarlet ornaments
And seal'd false bonds of love as oft as mine,
Robb'd others' beds' revenues of their rents.
Be it lawful I love thee as thou lov'st those
Whom thine eyes woo as mine importune thee!
Root pity in thy heart, that when it grows
Thy pity may deserve to pitied be.
    If thou dost seek to have what thou dost hide,
    By self example mayst thou be denied!

1 *thy dear virtue*] the virtue which you prize so highly 2 *sinful loving*] (on your part) 4 *it*] i.e. my sin/love 8 Robbed other women of what is due to them (sexually) and of what they would yield (i.e. children. *Revenues* is stressed on the second syllable) 9 May it be lawful for me to . . . 13 *what thou dost hide*] i.e. pity, which you do not show me 14 *self*] your own

143

Lo, as a careful housewife runs to catch
One of her feather'd creatures broke away,
Sets down her babe and makes all swift dispatch
In pursuit of the thing she would have stay,
Whilst her neglected child holds her in chase,
Cries to catch her whose busy care is bent
To follow that which flies before her face,
Not prizing her poor infant's discontent:
So runn'st thou after that which flies from thee,
Whilst I, thy babe, chase thee afar behind;
But if thou catch thy hope, turn back to me
And play the mother's part: kiss me, be kind.
  So will I pray that thou mayst have thy Will
  If thou turn back and my loud crying still.

1 *careful*] prudent, anxious; *housewife*] (pronounced 'hussif') 2 *feather'd creatures*] farmyard fowl (implicitly likened to 'your' befeathered gallants) 5 *holds her in chase*] chases her 6 *Cries*] weeps, shouts 8 *prizing*] paying attention to 11 *thy hope*] what you pursue 13 *Will*] (a pun on the name)

144

Two loves I have, of comfort and despair,
Which like two spirits do suggest me still.
The better angel is a man right fair,
The worser spirit a woman colour'd ill.
To win me soon to hell my female evil
Tempteth my better angel from my side,
And would corrupt my saint to be a devil,
Wooing his purity with her foul pride.
And whether that my angel be turn'd fiend
Suspect I may, yet not directly tell;
But being both from me, both to each friend,
I guess one angel in another's hell.
    Yet this shall I ne'er know, but live in doubt
    Till my bad angel fire my good one out.

1 Two people are the object of my love, one bringing comfort, the other despair 2 *suggest*] prompt, tempt; *still*] continually 3 *right fair*] proper and handsome 4 *colour'd ill*] i.e. with dark hair and eyes 5 *To win me soon to hell*] i.e. to bring me to despair 8 *pride*] splendour of beauty, arrogance 10 *directly*] certainly 11 *from me*] away from me; *both to each friend*] each a friend of the other 12 *hell*] sexual parts 14 *fire . . . out*] drive away by passing on venereal disease

146

Poor soul, the centre of my sinful earth,
[. . .] these rebel powers that thee array;
Why dost thou pine within and suffer dearth,
Painting thy outward walls so costly gay?
Why so large cost, having so short a lease,
Dost thou upon thy fading mansion spend?
Shall worms, inheritors of this excess,
Eat up thy charge? Is this thy body's end?
Then, soul, live thou upon thy servant's loss,
And let that pine to aggravate thy store.
Buy terms divine in selling hours of dross;
Within be fed, without be rich no more.
  So shalt thou feed on Death, that feeds on men,
  And Death once dead, there's no more dying then.

1 *sinful earth*] i.e. body 2 (The printer of the 1609 Quarto repeated the last three words of line 1 by mistake at the start of this line; the two syllables that should fill the blank cannot be reconstructed, but something like 'thrall to' may be supposed); *powers*] (of the body); *array*] line up for battle, dress 3 *dearth*] famine, lack 8 *thy charge*] what you have spent so much on, your responsibility; *end*] fate, purpose 9 *thy servant's*] i.e. your body's 10 *aggravate*] increase; *store*] stock 11 *terms divine*] time in heaven 12 *without*] outside, in the body

150

O, from what power hast thou this powerful might
With insufficiency my heart to sway,
To make me give the lie to my true sight
And swear that brightness doth not grace the day?
Whence hast thou this becoming of things ill,
That in the very refuse of thy deeds
There is such strength and warrantise of skill
That in my mind thy worst all best exceeds?
Who taught thee how to make me love thee more,
The more I hear and see just cause of hate?
O, though I love what others do abhor,
With others thou shouldst not abhor my state:
    If thy unworthiness rais'd love in me,
    More worthy I to be belov'd of thee.

2 *With insufficiency*] by means of weakness; *sway*] rule 3 *give . . . sight*] tell my eyes, which see true, that they lie 5 *becoming . . . ill*] power of making bad or ugly things look good 7 *warrantise of skill*] assurance of power to do

Index of First Lines